PAULO COELHO

Confessions
of a Pilgrim

HarperCollinsPublishers
77–85 Fulham Palace Road
Hammersmith, London W6 8JB

The HarperCollins website address is:
www.harpercollins.co.uk

First published by Editoral Planeta, S.A., 1999
This edition published by HarperCollins*Publishers*, 2001

9

© Juan Arias, 1999
English translation © Anne McLean, 2001

Juan Arias asserts the moral right to
be identified as the author of this work

A catalogue record for this book
is available from the British Library

ISBN 0 00 711 437 0

Printed in Great Britain by
Clays Ltd, St Ives plc

PAULO COELHO

Confessions of a Pilgrim

BY JUAN ARIAS

Translated from the Spanish by Anne McLean

'We are all pilgrims in search of the unknown.'

HarperCollins*Publishers*

Contents

About
Paulo Coelho

Paulo Coelho, one of the world's best-selling authors, was born in the Botafogo neighbourhood of Río de Janeiro, under the sign of Virgo, on 24 August, 1947. He was born – and feels proud to have been – on the same day, of the same month and under the same sign, although many years later, as his literary idol, Jorge Luis Borges. When he was still quite young, having first committed his poetry to memory, he took a bus from Río de Janeiro and travelled for forty-eight hours to Buenos Aires, in order to meet Borges in person. He found him after more than a few difficulties and stood mutely before him. He looked at him and thought, 'Idols don't speak,' and went back to Río.

He doesn't deny there is much of Borges in his works, beginning with *The Alchemist*, the book that brought him worldwide fame. Undoubtedly, it was the brilliant Argentinian who put the idea of becoming a writer into the head of the son of engineer Pedro Queima Coelho de Souza, when his father wanted him to be a lawyer. Later, he would be committed to a mental hospital for disobeying him about this.

In reality, the boy Paulo – who came into this world through a difficult birth, which led his profoundly religious mother, Lygia Araripe Coelho, to have him baptized in the clinic where he was born – always dreamt of an artistic career, something frowned upon in his upper-middle-class household. Perhaps, for this reason, he had trouble at school. He liked to read, not just Borges but Henry Miller as well, and grew fond of the theatre. His parents, seeing his lack of academic progress, sent him to the then strict Jesuit school, Colegio de San Ignacio, in Río de Janeiro, where he learned to be disciplined in life but where he also lost his religious faith. He didn't, however, lose his love of literature, in fact he won his first poetry contest at the school.

Coelho was always a nonconformist, a seeker after the new, leading him to try everything good and everything bad that appeared along the way. When, in the fever of '68, the guerrilla and hippy movements took hold, the future writer fell in love with Marx, Engels and Che Guevara. He took part in elections and demonstrations. He was involved in all the progressive movements and was part of the Peace and Love generation.

It was then that Coelho began to experience his crisis of faith and went off in search of new spiritual experiences, resorting to drugs, hallucinogens, sects and magic, travelling all over Latin America in the footsteps of Carlos Castaneda.

In the end, he heeded his father and registered in the Faculty of Law at the University of Río de Janeiro. But he soon dropped out to work in the theatre, his new dream. With the money he made as an actor, and after escaping from a mental hospital, he went to the United States, where fellow hippies helped him when he ran out of money.

Writing was still his passion, so he began to dabble in journalism and founded an alternative magazine called 2001. The magazine lasted only two issues but had an enormous importance for him because, as a result of one of the articles, he came into contact with the music producer Raúl Seixas, with whom he would eventually collaborate as a lyricist. It was his first moment of glory. The singer was working in many countries and Coelho began to make so much money from his lyrics that he bought five apartments. He also wrote for the Río newspaper *El Globo* until, in 1974, he published his first book, on the theatre in education.

These were also the years when he had his most intense experiences with black magic, as inspired by Aleister Crowley, one of the hardest and most difficult experiences of his life, which he speaks about in depth in this book. When he managed to free himself from the chains of black magic that were dragging him to the edge of the abyss, he had to go through another of life's cruel experiences: he was kidnapped and tortured by a group of paramilitaries during the Brazilian dictatorship.[1]

Almost miraculously, he escaped from the abduction and tortures with his life. He then decided to put a stop to the madness of drugs and black magic and embark on a normal life, working for several record companies. But, in 1976, the writing bug stirred within him again and he moved to England as correspondent for several Brazilian magazines and decided to write his life story, which he spent a year working on. However, before returning to

---

[1] The Brazilian military regime, which lasted from 1964 to 1985.

Brazil, he accidentally left the manuscript behind in a London pub and his autobiography remained unpublished.

After three failed marriages, in 1981 he married Cristina Oiticica, a painter with whom he would share the greatest successes of his life as a world famous writer. They are still happily married. But his passion for travel, in the search of his personal mission, was undiminished. With the money he had earned, they set out to travel the world for six months until, in Germany, in a concentration camp, he underwent a profound and intense spiritual experience that set off another change in his life, bringing him back to the Catholic beliefs of his parents. It was then, with his spiritual master, he spent fifty-five days walking the seven hundred kilometres of the ancient road to Santiago de Compostela, in the footsteps of the pilgrims of the Middle Ages.

The experience of the pilgrimage to Santiago drove him to publish what would be his first literary text: *Diary of a Magus* (later re-titled *The Pilgrimage*). After this would come his other books, from *The Alchemist* to the recent *Veronika Decides to Die*, establishing him as one of the ten best-selling authors in the world, an author who stirs up controversy and extremes of passion, but who continues, smiling and sure, on his path to awaken the lost taste for mystery and magic in the men and women at the beginning of this new millennium, overcoming tedium and helplessness in the bosom of a mechanized and bored society.

Coelho often says he has enough money for three reincarnations. He earns so much that he has committed four hundred thousand dollars a year of his author's royalties to a foundation that carries his name and which his wife, Cristina, administers. The money is used for the care of abandoned children in the worst slums of Río, for the poor and needy elderly, to promote the translation into other languages of Brazilian classics, and for the investigation of the fossil origins of his much-loved Brazil, which he considers the most magical country in the world because, as he says, in Brazil there is no difference between the sacred and the profane and no one is ashamed to believe in the spirit.

About the
Conversations

These conversations with Paulo Coelho took place in his Río de Janeiro home, overlooking the splendid Copacabana beach, at the beginning of July 1998, at the height of the World Cup in France, interrupted only so the writer could watch the matches he was covering for the French press.

During these long conversations, Coelho opened his soul and revealed, for the first time, painful moments from his past, such as the time he spent in the deserts of drugs, black magic and satanic worship, a mental hospital, prison and torture. At the end of the sessions, he stressed his desire not to have to talk about his life again for another twenty years.

My companion, the Brazilian writer and poet, Roseana Murray, took part in these encounters. At first they took place in the afternoons, after Coelho had taken his daily walk on the beach as soon as he woke up. Since he writes at night, he goes to bed at dawn, sleeps for the morning and spends the afternoon meeting people and going through his extensive correspondence – letters, faxes, e-mail, telephone calls – from all corners of the globe.

Because of this, our conversations were often interrupted by arriving messages. Sometimes these messages could be heard on the answering machine. Coelho would listen and, depending on the urgency of the matter, get up, or not, to answer. Once he said, 'Excuse me, but Boris Yeltsin is about to send a fax inviting me to Moscow.'

One afternoon he wanted to open that day's thick bundle of letters with us and tell us about them. He often gets letters from strangers, sometimes several pages long, telling him what they feel when reading his books, asking him the most diverse questions and confessing to him as to a benevolent magus. That day, among the dozens of letters, there was one from the Brazilian Minister of the Armed Forces. He told him he'd read his book *Manual of the Warriors of Light.* 'This isn't normal,' said Coelho. 'Important people don't usually bother to write, though when I meet them they tell me they read my books, like Shimon Peres did in Switzerland during the Davos congress, a meeting of the leading international economists, which I was invited to address this year.'

Speaking about that meeting in Davos, to which only Coelho and the President of the Republic, Fernando Enrique Cardoso, were invited from Brazil, the writer would say that the 'real magic tricks' were performed by economists and financiers these days, not by poor professional magicians.

The view over the sea at Copacabana, which took on every shade of blue as the afternoon turned to evening, gave Coelho frequent recourse to images of the sea in reply to our questions. He always answered in Spanish, a language he loves and speaks fluently. The author of *The Alchemist* is not a man of half measures; rather, he is a man of extremes, a passionate man, accustomed to what he calls 'the good fight,' someone who doesn't mind arguing, always incredibly straightforward, though never entirely sure of anything, who knows how to listen and is able to admit he could be wrong.

One afternoon there was an hour-long interruption because a representative of his Brazilian publisher arrived with a professional photographer to take a series of photos for the launch of his novel, *Veronika Decides to Die*. He wanted us to stay for the photo session and he was immortalized in every conceivable position, including barefoot, sitting cross-legged at his computer desk. Watching the mastery of the photographer, it became clear these would be the best photos ever taken of him. The editor commented, 'So, what'll we do with the other pictures?' Coelho answered, 'You could send them out to the provincial newspapers.' My partner, Roseana, affectionately told him off, 'Paulo, you're doing just what the First World does to us – sending their rubbish.' Coelho didn't think twice, 'You're right, Roseana,' and he asked for the old photos not to be used and that the new ones be sent to provincial papers as well.

A few days later I told the theologian Leonard Boff about the incident, in his house in the middle of the Itaipava forest, near Petrópolis. Boff has always defended Coelho against his critics because he believes his books awaken a love of mystery and spirit in a cold, distracted world. Upon hearing about the photo episode, Boff commented, 'I always appreciate people who are not afraid to acknowledge their mistakes. It takes strength of character.'

During the final days, the conversations took place at night. Coelho, used to working just as most people start to go to sleep, felt fresh as a daisy. He was even more communicative. We only stopped when the rest of us were overcome by tiredness. Had it been up to him, we would have carried on all night. There was only one moment when the writer took a break: at midnight. It is a ritual time for him, as is six o'clock in the evening, when the sun sets. He would ask for a few seconds of silence for a moment of prayer.

Sometimes others participated in those night talks, which were more intimate, more confessional. His wife, Cristina, sensitive and tactful, always asked if she could stay to listen. At one point, Coelho said to her, 'Listen very closely, because you're going to hear things that not even you have heard before, now that I've decided to bare my soul, so everyone can know who I've been and who I am, and won't invent false personas for me.'

At night we held our conversations in the dining room, on the opposite side of the house. On the table were plates of ham and cheese *tapas*, Spanish-style, accompanied by a superb Italian wine. The perfect atmosphere for confidences, especially as no one from outside interrupted, because at that hour the fax, phone and several computers were silent. The house was thick with a silence that was absent during the day, because of the world's relentless pursuit of its most popular writer.

Three young Spanish university students participated in one of the night-time discussions: sisters Paula and Ana, and María, a friend of theirs. Their parents worked for an international company based in Río de Janeiro; they were studying in Madrid and came to see their parents for the holidays. I met them on the aeroplane, coming from Madrid. When they heard that I was going to do a book with the writer Paulo Coelho, their eyes lit up. And each of them showed me which one of his books they were reading: *Brida*,[2] *The Fifth Mountain* and *By the River Piedra I Sat Down and Wept*. I could see in their eyes that meeting him would be a dream come true.

Coelho, who is very sensitive to certain signs, interpreted my meeting those three young students, reading his books on their way to Río, as a good omen for the task at hand. The writer's encounter with the three young students was not just emotive, but lively, bold and sincere. It also included an exceptional presence: that of Mauro Salles, advertising executive, intellectual and poet, a very respected personality in Brazil, whom Coelho considers a spiritual father figure. They usually see in the New Year together, along with their wives, in the solitude of the grotto at Lourdes. Salles attended Coelho's meeting with the three young women, sitting among them, taking notes on what was said and joining in as an equal.

---

[2] *Brida* is not at present available in an English language edition.

Coelho, writer and magus, is very faithful to certain rituals and doesn't hide this fact. So, on the night he decided to touch on his painful past experiences with black magic and satanic rituals, he turned off all the lights in the house and lit the room with candles. 'I feel better talking about these things this way,' he told us. And he told it all, almost without me having to ask questions, as if he were talking to himself, remembering old wounds to his soul.

One of the moments of greatest emotional tension happened when, relating the spiritual experience he underwent at Dachau, which radically changed his life, he burst into tears. After a few moments silence, to play it down, he said, 'Perhaps I've had too much to drink.' And the moment of greatest pleasure was when his wife, Cristina, picked up a white feather from underneath the table and handed it to her husband. 'Paulo, look what was down there.' And she put the feather on the table. Coelho brightened, took his wife's hand and, deeply moved, said, 'Thank you, Cristina!' For him, the fortuitous appearance of a white feather at his side is a sign of the impending birth of a new book. And, at that moment, we were just coming to the end of this book.

He wanted us to finish our conversations in the same place as we'd begun, in his bedroom, facing Copacabana beach, in the gentle sunlight of the Río winter. I asked him if he considered himself a magus as well as a writer, and he answered, 'Yes, I am a magus, but so is everyone who knows how to read the hidden language of things in pursuit of their personal destiny.'

In this book I have tried to maintain the informal tone of the friendly conversations with the writer. Conversations that, at times, had their polemical moments and, at others, were confessional in the intimate atmosphere that had developed. In a gesture of trust, Coelho has not wanted to revise the text, leaving me complete responsibility for it. Thus, any error it may contain is entirely my own.

My heartfelt thanks to Mauro Salles, the person who knows Paulo Coelho better than anyone else. His moral and knowledgeable support, so generously offered, helped me to understand more profoundly the complex and rich personality of the Brazilian writer.

I would like to assure readers of Coelho, old and new, that they were, at all times, the object of the writer's attention. He had them in mind each time he uttered an opinion or revealed an unknown facet of his rich and busy life. They are, then, the authentic audience of this book.

CHAPTER I

Omens

❧

*'Omens are an alphabet you develop
to talk to the world's soul.'*

❧

Paulo Coelho is more than a writer, something many of his literary critics have not understood. He is multifaceted, an emblematic person. His books are more than pure fiction, which is why they unleash conflicting passions and unbreakable bonds. It also follows that his relationships with his readers are not typical writer–reader relationships. I had first-hand evidence of this in Río de Janeiro, at the Bank of Brazil Cultural Centre. Coelho was to read from *The Fifth Mountain* as part of a series of readings, and the public – some thousand people – could ask questions. Well, in spite of itself, the cultural event turned into a group psychotherapy session. The questions were meant to be submitted on paper but this plan went out the window; people stood up to speak directly to him, confessing in public how his books had changed their lives. They wanted to know everything about him. They embraced him when they came up for the book signing, which lasted several hours.

Coelho's life is now fundamentally centred on being a writer, something he's struggled towards his whole life and has achieved beyond his own expectations. But he is a writer who likes to immerse himself in life, peer at it, read the secret alphabet of the universe and the omens that are sent to us, like coded messages.

Our encounter in Río de Janeiro, began with one of those omens. The first meeting was scheduled for two o'clock in the afternoon. It had been planned for six months. When I arrived at his house, the door-man told me he had not yet returned from his morning walk along the beach, a walk he takes each day to enjoy a drink of coconut milk and greet the people who, recognizing him, come over for a chat. I sat down to wait for him in the bar next door to his house. He arrived half an hour late, smiling but worried. Before I'd even turned on the tape recorder, he rushed to tell me what had just happened, because he considered it one of those 'omens' that oblige you to reflect on life. It made such a profound impression on him that he used it as the subject of one of his Sunday columns in the Río de Janeiro newspaper *O Globo*, entitled 'A Man Lying on the Ground' which follows:

'On the 1st of July, at five minutes past three, a man in his fifties was lying on the pavement near Copacabana beach. I walked past, took a quick look and carried on in the direction of a stall where I go each day to drink coconut milk.

Being from Río, I've seen hundreds, perhaps thousands, of men, women and children lying on the ground. And, as a person who travels widely, I've seen the same scene in every country I've visited – from wealthy Switzerland to wretched Romania – and I've seen them at every season of the year: in the freezing winters of Madrid, New York or Paris, where they dwell near the warm air that comes out of the subway entrances, on the burning ground of Lebanon, between buildings destroyed by war. People lying on the ground – drunk, exposed, tired – are not a novelty in our lives.

I drank my coconut milk. I had to go straight back, for I had an appointment with Juan Arias, from the Spanish newspaper *El País*.

On my way back I saw the man still lying there in the sun, and everyone walking by as I had done: taking a look and carrying on.

It happened that – although I hadn't noticed – my soul had become tired of seeing this scene so many times. When I walked past that man for the second time, something stronger within me led me to kneel down and try to help him up.

He didn't respond. I turned his head to one side and saw blood near his temples. So, was it something serious? I cleaned the blood off with my T-shirt: it didn't look too severe.

At that moment the man began to murmur a few words like: 'Tell them not to hit me.' Well then, he was alive, so I had to get him up and call the police.

I stopped the first man who walked by and asked him to help me get him into the shade, between the pavement and the sand of the beach. He dropped everything and came to help me. His soul must have grown tired of observing that same scene too.

Once we'd got the man into the shade, I headed for home. I knew there was a police station nearby and I could ask for help there. But before I got there, I ran into two police officers. 'There is an injured man in front of number such and such,' I told them. 'I moved him onto the sand, you've got to get an ambulance.' The policemen told me they'd see to it. So, I had fulfilled my duty. Good deed of the day! The problem was now in someone else's hands, they would have to take care of it. I thought the Spanish journalist would be arriving at my house.

I hadn't taken ten steps when a foreigner came over. He spoke to me in a barely intelligible Portuguese. 'I'd already told the police about that man,' he said to me, 'but they told me if it wasn't a robbery it was none of their concern.'

I didn't even let the man finish speaking. I turned back to the police officers, convinced they'd recognize me as a person who writes in the newspapers and appears on television. I went back to them under the false impression that success can solve many problems. 'Have you got some authority?' one of them asked me, seeing that I was requesting help in a more incisive manner. He hadn't the faintest idea who I might be. 'No,' I told them, 'but let's get this taken care of right now.'

I was scruffily dressed, in cut-off jeans, my T-shirt stained with that man's blood, and sweaty. To them I was just an average, anonymous man, with no more authority than that coming from my weariness of seeing people lying on the ground, for years of my life, without being able to do anything for them.

And that changed everything. There comes a time when you find yourself beyond any fear. There comes a moment when your eyes suddenly see things another way, and people understand you're talking seriously. The policemen accompanied me and went to phone an ambulance.

On my way back home, I thought of the three lessons of that experience:

a) we can all stop an action when we are still pure; *b)* there will always be someone to tell you, 'okay, now you've started, see it through to the end.' And finally, *c)* we are all authorities when we are absolutely sure of what we're doing.

— The subject of omens, of the kind you just lived through at the beach before meeting us, how to recognize them, and what they can mean to our lives, is a recurring theme in your books. But how do you know when it's a true omen? It would be easy to read signs into everything …

— You're right, because in trying to read omens into everything we could end up paranoid. Look, right now I see a rose embroidered on Roseana's handbag, and over there by the computer I've got a Saint Theresa of Lisieux and a rose. Now, I could see this as a clear sign of complicity towards Saint Theresa, but you could drive yourself crazy, because you might see a Galaxy bar and think you had to talk about galaxies. And it's not that.

— So what is an omen then?

— Omens are a language, it's the alphabet we develop to speak to the world's soul, or the universe's, or God's, whatever name you want to give it. Like any alphabet, it is individual, you only learn it by making mistakes, and that keeps you from globalizing the spiritual quest.

— *What do you understand by globalizing the spiritual quest?*

— Look, to my way of thinking, in the next hundred years the tendency of humanity is going to veer towards the search for spirituality. I see that people are already more open to this theme than they were during the last century. We've started to realize that the saying about religion being the opiate of the masses doesn't hold, especially since those who said it had probably never even tried opium.

What happens is that when people start becoming involved with religion they're getting into uncharted waters. And when we find ourselves sinking in an unfamiliar sea, fear takes over and at that moment we grab onto the nearest person for help. We all need to make contact with others, to commune with the soul of others.

But at the same time we need to stand on our own two feet, walk with our own legs, like when you walk the pilgrim's road to Santiago. You start in darkness, not knowing what you'll find, although wanting to find clues to meet up with yourself, with your destiny. And these clues come to us by way of a richer alphabet, which allows us to intuit what we should or should not do.

— *But don't you think there's a danger we'll see the omens that suit us or that could take us away from the true path? How do you reach this certainty that it is a true sign?*

– No. What happens is that at the beginning we hardly believe in anything; at a second stage we think we're mistaken; at the third, everything seems to be an omen, and then, only at the end, when an omen crosses our path over and over again without being sought out, you realize you're facing a language that goes beyond reality.

– Could you give a personal example of something that's happened to you recently that you've interpreted as an omen?

– I told you before that I have Saint Theresa of Lisieux over there by my computer. It might strike you as strange, but my devotion to the French saint, who died when she was almost a child, came about as a result of the process I just described. I had had nothing to do with her. But, gradually, she began to appear in my life. I read a book of hers and my first reaction was pity: she seemed like a poor hysteric to me.

– To digress for a moment. The first book written in France on the handwriting of the Church's great saints caused a scandal. The conclusion was that, had they not followed the religious path, those great personages, venerated as saints, would have become either outstanding criminals or outstanding prostitutes. The explanation the handwriting expert gave was that they had such strong person-alities that, had they not sublimated their urges with religion, they could have been great murderers or prostitutes.

– No doubt about it. And it doesn't only apply to saints. They say the best surgeons have to have a large dose of suppressed sadism, or else they wouldn't be able to operate well. Just as they say a good psychiatrist has to have at least a pinch of madness.

– *And writers?*

(Paulo Coelho laughs and says, 'I think we writers have something of the criminal in us too, especially the ones who write mystery and crime novels.')

– *Getting back to your Saint Theresa. How did all that start?*

– It started last year, a few weeks before I met you in Madrid. I was coming back from Germany. I'd been asked to be godfather to a child and the priest who performed the baptism started talking to me about Saint Theresa during the meal and gave me one of her books. I left it in the hotel, you know how awkward it is to travel with books, and even worse if they don't interest you. But before leaving, I asked the priest to bless me because I was about to begin a very long tour. He took me to a corner of the hotel and blessed me. But then he knelt and said, 'Now you bless me.' 'Me?' I asked, not understanding what was going on, because I knew it was priests who bless people not the other way around. But he insisted and, so he wouldn't be displeased, I blessed him.

That's where it all started. Before the Book Fair someone came up to me – I'd thrown away the book the priest had given me without reading it – and said, 'I have a message for you from Saint Theresa.' I'll tell you, by the way, that I've reached a point in my life where I believe everything. If someone says to me, 'Come on, let's go watch horses fly,' I go. My first instinct is to give people the benefit of the doubt, although, I have to say, I don't like liars. But I've seen so many miracles in my life that when the stranger told me he had a message for me from Saint Theresa, I believed him.

– But there must have been more to it than that for you to understand that this saint was going to be important in your life.

– Of course, because from that moment on I began to find things out I'd never suspected. For example, my father told me – my father who had me committed to a mental hospital when I was young – that my mother had always been very devoted to this saint. Right now they're making a film about my travels, it's a Franco-Canadian-American co-production, and in Japan the cameraman said to me – we'd never mentioned the subject – 'I'm making a film about Saint Theresa, because she's the saint of my devotion, can you talk to me about her? I know you don't believe in Saint Theresa, but ...' 'What do you mean I don't believe in Saint Theresa!', I said. These are omens. I'm telling you this story because at the beginning you start off denying and later, when the omens keep showing up, they do so in a very individual and unmistakable language.

— But what happens if you're wrong and you follow the trail of a false omen? Couldn't this destroy your life?

— It is a sensitive, important matter. For me, the danger does not consist of the possibility of making a mistake and following an omen that turns out to be false. For me, the greatest dangers in the spiritual search are gurus, masters, fundamentalism: what I referred to before as the globalization of spirituality. When someone comes and tells you: God is this, God is that, my God is stronger than yours. That's how wars start. The only way to escape all that is to understand that the spiritual search is a personal responsibility that you can't transfer or entrust to others. It's better to make a mistake following omens that your conscience tells you are guiding you, than to let others decide your destiny. All this should not be taken as a criticism of religion, which I consider a very important aspect of human life.

— So what does religion mean to you?

— I see it as a group of people who find a collective way to worship. I said worship, not obey. They are two very different things. This group of people could worship Buddha, Allah, God, the father of Jesus, it doesn't matter. What matters is that, at the moment we connect with mystery, we feel more united, more open to life and we realize we're not alone in the world, that we don't live in isolation. That is religion for me, not a set of rules and orders imposed by others.

— *But, if I'm not mistaken, you accept the dogma of the Roman Catholic Church, to which you returned after your period of atheism.*

— A discussion of dogma could go on for a long while. You accept a dogma because you want to accept it, not because it's imposed on you. When I was a boy I said, without an ounce of understanding, the same as everyone else: that María had conceived without sin, that Jesus was God, that God was the Trinity. Later, I learned about right-wing theology, liberation theology, all of them. They are forms that change and evolve. But I'm fifty and the dogmas are centuries old. According to Jung, dogmas that are so absurd in appearance constitute the clearest, most magical and most inspired manifestation of human thinking, because they are beyond conscious thought.

These days, no matter how absurd it may appear, I accept dogma freely into my heart. Not because it's imposed, not because I feel forced into it, as in the past, but because I try to be humble before mystery. Deep down, all religions have their dogmas, which are paradigms of the most profound, arcane mystery. To me that seems beautiful, because there's no reason that something I don't understand rationally should not be true. Mystery exists.

— *The problem is that religions try to impose their dogmas through fear of eternal punishment.*

— I lived through that in my childhood. That's why I gave up on religion and became an atheist. I was convinced that Catholicism was the worst thing in the world, just another sect. That's why I had to make such a long journey before coming back to it. I'm not saying that Catholicism is better than other religions, but it is in my cultural roots, in my blood. For me it was a personal and free choice. I could have chosen Islam or Buddhism, or nothing. But I felt I needed something more than atheism in my life and I chose Catholicism as a way of communing with mystery along with other people who believe as I do. And this has nothing to do with the priest who says mass. Dogma is something beyond rites, the search for mystery is a search for great freedom.

— *But don't you find it problematic that those dogmas you accept as a way of connecting with the divine also come from an institution that created the Inquisition, that acted against those who didn't accept their dogmas?*

– Yes, and from a Church that still denies women the right to full participation in ecclesiastical life.

– An institution that has abused power so often and shackled so many consciences.

– In Latin America it caused much suffering, and in Spain too, no?

– And in spite of that, you don't have problems …?

– No, because I know how to distinguish between the essence of religion and the attitudes of its followers, who might be good or bad and who can abuse religion. I see religion as a group of people who make up a living body that develops and includes all its miserable and sublime aspects.

– If I've understood you correctly, what you salvage from religion is mystery and the communion between believers.

– Yes. I'm interested in the people who believe in that mystery, not who celebrate the mystery, that could be undignified. Mystery is beyond those who celebrate it. In the parable of the good Samaritan, Jesus reproaches the conduct of the Levite who walks past the injured man and doesn't stop. The Levite was the religious man of that time. In contrast, he praises the Samaritan who helps the injured man. And the Samaritans were the atheists of their day.

— Do you think every spiritual quest requires an established Church?

— No. Just the opposite. You have to be very careful when you join a Church to not let them try to take over what is your responsibility. What I believe is that religion itself, not what is sometimes made out of religions, is not in contradiction with a personal spiritual quest. The important thing is to create a large empty space within yourself, get rid of the superfluous, know how to live the essential, always be on the way.

I remember in my hippie days we had our houses jam-packed with stuff: posters, records, books, magazines, all kinds of things. There weren't any empty spaces. I've freed myself from all that now. As you can see, my house is very big, but it's empty. I just keep a few symbolic things. Even my books are hidden away, because I don't like to exhibit what I'm reading or what I've just read.

— I'm very interested in the importance you ascribe to emptiness. There's a lovely poem by Lao-tsê that says:

> *We put thirty spokes together and call it a wheel;*
> *But it is on the space where there is nothing that the*
> *   usefulness of the wheel depends.*

We turn clay to make a vessel;
But it is on the space where there is nothing that the
    usefulness of the vessel depends.
We pierce doors and windows to make a house;
And it is on these spaces where there is nothing that the
    usefulness of the house depends.
Therefore just as we take advantage of what is, we should
    recognize the usefulness of what is not.

— That's a lovely poem. As a matter of fact, I am now trying to simplify my life to the greatest degree possible, reduce it to its essential. Even when I travel I take only the absolute necessities so I feel light and free.

Buddha said, 'It's very easy for the impotent man to take a vow of chastity and for the poor to renounce wealth.' I haven't taken a vow of chastity, but, on the other hand, since I travel so much, bit by bit I'm discovering how simple life is and how little we need to live happily. In fact, when I travel I take a tiny little suitcase. And I've realized this minimal luggage suits me just as well for long trips as for short ones. No one can feel full if they haven't first been able to empty themselves from within, as all the great mystics of all the great religions have told us.

— *You emphasize that man must follow a spiritual path, whatever it may be, because he can't be fully happy with just material things, no matter how interesting.*

But, don't you think that sometimes it is fear that leads people to take refuge in spirituality?

– No. Why? In every era men have searched for the unknown, for what is not evident, tangible and material. They've searched in thousands of ways, sometimes making mistakes, in fits and starts, but the best men and women have always been pilgrims in search of the unknown.

– *And precisely because the field of what man has discovered is ever increasing, they tend to search for what remains unknown, whatever that may be, is that it?*

– Exactly. What happens is that sometimes we live trapped by the fallacy of utopias: the Marxist utopia tried to change everything by changing the structures of society and getting rid of capitalism. It didn't manage it. Another utopia is the Freudian one, which subordinates the cure of the soul to the return to the past. And a third utopia is that of conservatism, which tries to solve everything by leaving things as they are, immobile, changing nothing except the minimum to keep things as they are. Now all these twentieth-century utopias have failed, at least for the most part.

– *What's the alternative?*

– The great quest, the path towards somewhere as yet unknown, a rough sea, mined with dangers, with tricks, gurus, masters who want to impose on us their vision of things and the world.

You said earlier that sometimes people go towards a spiritual quest out of fear, but out of fear people also stay sitting on the beach without attempting anything. Humanity is at a crossroads. On one side, the already familiar course of conservatism, crystallization, legal regulation, imposition, religion as a legal system of conduct; on the other side, the dark forest, the unknown, the new, true creative culture, the search for questions that could still have answers, the acceptance of life as an adventure of the spirit.

– There is a critic of yours who claims that in this new century and millennium no one will need your books anymore.

– Curiously, the ending of a century changes nothing for me. It's a convention. And soon we won't be talking about the millennium anymore, because we'll have seen how nothing has changed and everything's still the same. Those who criticize me perhaps expected something special was going to happen, while I was sure nothing would. The problems we had at midnight that night, we still had on the first day of the new millennium. The universe carries on and men still have the same fears, the same hopes and desires to keep searching for something that quenches their thirst for the infinite that's never left them in all these centuries, which is the impulse to search after the unknown.

(At this moment in the conversation, a helicopter crosses the sky over beach trailing a gigantic advert for the new Río de Janeiro subway station which, after a fifteen-year wait, has finally arrived fifty metres from the mythic Copacabana beach. Coelho explains they'd asked him to sponsor the advert and allow them to use a phrase of his, but he'd refused because it would have meant publicity for politicians.)

– Getting back to the subject of the spiritual quest, is it true that you see it as a great adventure?

– It is the great adventure, the most exciting thing we've got. In 1492, in Granada – that city I find so magical – all logic led that country towards Africa; Granada was re-conquered. They had expelled Boabdil, the last of the Moors, what would their next adventure be? Cross the strait and head for Africa. But a man who was there at the surrender of the last Moor said, 'What Africa? We already know Africa, I want money to go to the Indies.' 'What do you mean the Indies, man?' Africa was the logical place. That's why I don't much like following logic, I prefer the philosophy of paradox, which very often triumphs over logic and evidence. The fact is, that man, Christopher Columbus, was there that year and didn't want to leave it till the next year, and he didn't do it the previous year. He did it the same year as the re-conquest of Granada. On 12 October of that very year, 1492, Columbus got to America and all the flow of Spain's energy, which logically should have been flowing towards Africa, changed course towards America.

– *And thanks to that, here we are.*

– Perhaps. We can't know that, but the history of Spain would certainly have been different. The fact of the matter is that a man – not a political system or military logic – a pig-headed adventurer, was able to change the course of everything the politicians of the day expected.

These are things that change the world. And today, the same thing still happens, on a large and small scale. Of course, today it's harder for one man alone to change the direction of the world. But when all those adventurers who still believe in searching after the unknown are put together and those who let themselves be carried by the energy of their spirit, without feeling tormented by rigid Cartesian logic, they end up creating a critical mass able to change things. More spiritual adventurers exist today than most people think. They travel unknown seas and they are the ones who, in the end, without knowing how, suddenly change the winds of history.

— Is it possible to recognize these spiritual adventurers from among the mass of those content with their daily crust of bread?

— Yes, because their eyes shine with the light of enthusiasm. I wrote a book called *Manual for the Warriors of the Light*. It's about normal people who still believe in the unknown. They are masters without being masters. The truth is we are now all disciples and masters many times a day. Like the foreigner who alerted me to the police officers' attitude towards the injured man on Copacabana beach. He was my master because he made me recognize I could do something because I am Brazilian. We are all masters. Warriors of the light, the new spiritual adventurers, recognize each other because they have all the defects, vanities, feelings of guilt all mortals have, but at the same time they also have something else which is this fire in their eyes. They experience things and life with enthusiasm, although without feeling themselves to be different or privileged.

— It's an antidote against the defeatism and solitude that generally invades contemporary man, who thinks there is no longer any space for new, out of the ordinary adventures.

— Yes, because they know they're not alone. I think one of the reasons for my books' success, which many find hard to understand, lies in that they help these spiritual adventurers recognize themselves as such. Because my books are full of omens. I don't write about omens, only in one paragraph in *The Alchemist*, but everyone understands exactly what I'm talking about.

– *And why is that?*

– Because we're all inside the same vibration. The writer is only one more companion on this adventure. What novelties do my books contain? None. What do I share with my readers? My life, my experiences. So a reader in Japan, who possesses a very different culture from mine, tells me, 'I already knew that, I didn't have it at a conscious level, but I sensed you were talking about me.'

Now with my novel, *Veronika Decides to Die*, which touches on the themes of madness and suicide, I made ten copies of the manuscript and gave them to various people to read. And, much to my surprise, each and every one of them had had a brush with suicide or madness in their families. I got a fax from England saying, 'I received your book. I loved it. I think the only time in my life when I felt far from God was when I tried to kill myself, but I survived.' It was signed Amelia. Well, Amelia is a woman who's been working with me for over twenty years, and I had absolutely no idea she'd ever attempted suicide.

– *In other words, the writer as catalyst for the experiences of others.*

— Yes, a catalyst, not a transformational element. The function of a catalyst is precisely that, not to mix with the elements but to allow them to become manifest. People discover things as they go along. Someone is studying Law, but realizes what they enjoy is gardening. I get thousands of letters from people who would like to change careers and devote themselves to gardening. Some say their families think the best thing to be is an engineer, but what they'd love to do is be able to work in a garden, in the fresh air, in contact with nature.

— *That's all very nice. But has it never occurred to you that someone could fail for wanting to follow your message.*

— Yes, me.

— *That's just a joke.*

— Okay, now joking aside. In reality, I'm not sending messages to anybody. In my books I just tell what's happened to me in my life. I say that this happened to me, but I don't add, 'You do the same'. No, I talk about my tragedy, my mistakes, of how I came through them, but I don't say that that's the solution for everyone, because every life is different and personal. In fact, if we lined up all the human beings on the planet we wouldn't find two identical.

I don't believe in collective messages, I believe in a catalysing, incendiary element. For example, I try to make it clear, through my own experience, that failing is not the same as being defeated. They fail who don't even try to fight their battle and they are defeated those who are able to struggle. And this defeat is no shame. It can be a trampoline to new victories. And, as José Saramago said so well in your book, *Possible Love*, there's no such thing as a definitive defeat or a definitive victory, because today's defeat could become tomorrow's victory.

— You declare yourself a believer. Who is God to you?

— An experience of faith. And no more. Because I consider defining God to be a trap. I was asked that question during a conference. I said, 'I don't know. God doesn't mean the same thing to me as God does to you.' And the auditorium erupted in applause. It's what people feel, that there isn't a God suitable for everyone, because it's something very personal.

— Leonardo Boff often says God is a 'great passion'.

— And in that sense, it is the same for everyone, because we are all able to cherish and conceive of a great passion.

— What then is an atheist to your way of thinking?

– For me, the formal act of believing or not believing in God changes nothing. I know atheists who live their lives a thousand times better than many who call themselves believers. Because sometimes the believer is tempted to turn into the judge of his fellow due to the simple fact of his belief in God. For me, an atheist is someone who answers to God only through works. As Saint James the Apostle said: what allows us to recognize ourselves as God's children are deeds, not our professions of faith. 'Show me your works and I'll show you your faith,' he said.

On the other hand, those of us who call ourselves believers have to confess that our faith is always very fragile. I believe today, for example, that my faith is strong, and tonight this certainty may have vanished. Faith is not a straight line.

– *The Sicilian writer Leonardo Sciascia used to say that sometimes he believed in the pavement and once he'd crossed the street he no longer believed in it.*

– Exactly. The difference is the believer has a certain conviction in the existence of something beyond, although often doesn't feel that faith.

– *At one point in these conversations you said that when you connect with the centre of energy you feel pleasure. What is pleasure for you?*

CHAPTER II

Mental Hospital, Prison and Torture

꧁꧂

'The worst thing I discovered in the asylum was that I could choose madness and live a quiet life without working.'

'Prison was first-hand experience of hatred, cruelty and total impotence. It was a thousand times worse than the mental hospital.'

꧁꧂

conserva
came int
quite lib
her eyes
open-mi
began to
and tradi
family.

— *Jesuits a*

— Not th
excellent
of religio
that, in c
soon as I
searched
believers.
Marx, Eng

— *But you e*

— When I
convinced
Catholic

The future writer's youth was not easy, but was rich in very diverse experiences, some of them cruel in the extreme, like being committed to a mental hospital and later suffering inprisonment, where he was tortured by a group of paramilitaries during the Brazilian dictatorship.

He was always a rebellious boy and young man, eager for experience, loyal son of '68, a time of openness and madness, always in search of something that would fill him from within, never allowing himself to be dominated by familial or social conventions. He was a self-professed non-conformist, although able to admit his mistakes when he made them and also capable of backing away from his excesses. As he confesses in these conversations, he never felt hatred or rancour towards his parents, who had him committed to a mental hospital three times when he was practically a child, convinced they were doing it for his own good.

— *What was your childhood like? Have you any brothers or sisters?*

— I have one sister who is a chemical engineer. I was the eldest by a whole generation and the most rebellious. I began to understand the truth of life, which is the following: whatever you do, if you're the eldest sibling, you'll always get blamed for everything that happens around you. You're always the victim. At first, that bothered me a lot, because, of course, there were things that weren't my fault, then one day I said to myself, 'Okay, if this is the way it is, I'm going to do everything I feel like.' That's how rebellious I was against injustice.

— What are

— It's odd
Botafogo,
I've lived r
believe an
even asked
to other (
mother as
opened my
that was as

— What mem

— My fath
mother ha
alive; he is
greatly.

— Did you g(

— Yes. I re
Sunday, bu
go on Frid
how the Je

completely convinced that was not the way, that theirs was a right-wing God, with no feminine side, a rigorous God, merciless, without compassion or mystery. At the same time I started to experiment with all the other religions and sects, especially the Eastern ones. I tried them all: Hare Krishna, Buddhism, Yogic philosophy, everything. I started to go to mass regularly again, only after making the pilgrimage to Santiago.

— You were restless.

— Totally. And after that I went back to atheism, after a terrible experience with black magic. I'll tell you about that later.

— What did you study at university?

— I studied Law, but only because I was obliged to. I didn't finish. Until finishing secondary school and the entrance exam for university, I had my rebelliousness totally under control, oppressed by my parents, society and the general atmosphere. But when I went off the rails, I exploded completely. That happened when I started university, but before that there was a point when I couldn't get anywhere with my studies, I spent three years in the last year of secondary school, I didn't finish, I couldn't get out of there until at last my family paid for me to pass the year and I passed. Just like that.

– *When you erupted that way, what was your family's reaction?*

– When I first went off, they had me committed to a mental hospital, like a madman.

– *How could they have someone sane committed to a mental hospital?*

– It was possible then. But anyway, my parents managed it. They had me committed three times because I kept escaping. Since that asylum still exists, recently, I tried to find out what reasons they used to get me locked up with the insane. And I was surprised by the banality of the motivations. In the medical report it says I was irritable, I harassed people politically, I was doing steadily worse in school, my mother thought I had sexual problems, I hadn't matured sufficiently for my age and when I wanted something I tried to get it by every possible means, which revealed increasingly radical and extremist attitudes.

– *How did you feel inside?*

– Look, I was seventeen years old. The only thing I wanted to do was write; I'd already started working as a reporter for a newspaper, and I'd just finished reading the complete works of Oscar Wilde. I was an idealist at heart and deep down I thought that for someone who wanted to be a writer, it was only right to have to undergo all experiences, even the mental hospital, which had been the fate of so many writers and artists, starting with Van Gogh. I saw it as part of my personal legend, of my yearning for adventure. I wrote poetry in the asylum, but I ended up escaping because I was very aware I wasn't mad; what I wanted was to live everything to the fullest, do everything I liked. Some people believe I was put in there because of drugs. Not at all. I hadn't even tried any drugs at that point. My experience with narcotics started much later, when I was almost twenty.

— What did you learn from being in the midst of the insane without being insane yourself?

— I want to be very honest with you. I think the big danger of madness is not madness itself, but the habit of madness. What I discovered during the time I spent in the asylum is that I could choose madness and spend my whole life without working, doing nothing, pretending to be mad. It was a very strong temptation, a great deal of my experience in that place can be found in *Veronika Decides to Die*.

The experience of the mental hospital demonstrated this: by the third day I was already saying, 'Well, I'm getting used to this, it's not so bad; I'm even comfortable and protected from the problems on the outside.' It was like a maternal womb that gave you tranquillity.

– *How did you get along with the inmates?*

– With the insane? They all seemed normal to me. They had moments of rage, just as you and I do in normal life. There were, in fact, a few schizophrenics who had lost contact with reality, but only three or four. I talked with the rest, we discussed philosophy, books, everything. We had a television and we could listen to music and we had lots of fun.

– *And the electric shocks?*

– That wasn't so nice, but you don't really feel much either. They were terrible, terrifying when they put them on my genitals during the torture by the paramilitaries, when I was kidnapped years later. That was painful, humiliating and mortifying. It was horrible.

– *The first time you were committed they let you out for good behaviour. But the second time, according to the medical records, you escaped from the asylum How did you manage it?*

– I was locked up on the ninth floor, I couldn't get out, they considered me dangerously insane; there were inmates who were allowed out. They gave me a lot of medication, electric shocks. I was shut up on that floor for almost two months, without seeing the sun; that almost drove me really crazy. There was a lift and a lift attendant who took you up or down, then one day I just got into the lift with him and other people, went down, got off and, incredibly, I sat down by the door, free. It was like a Kafka story.

— It's all very symbolic, you were a prisoner but in reality you weren't.

— It's a terrible symbolism. There is a Kafka story that tells of a person who comes up to the door of a castle and asks, 'May I enter?' The guard doesn't answer, and at the end of his life, he goes back and says to the guard, 'Why wouldn't you let me go in?' And the guard, who's old as well, replies, 'But I never said no. You asked me and I couldn't talk, why didn't you go in?' The same thing happened to me in the asylum: I went down in the elevator just as I was, in pyjamas, and, of course, I didn't go back to get anything; I had no money, nothing. I walked to a friend's house, he gave me a guitar, a bit of money, and when I left there I said to myself, 'Now what do I do?' and I started travelling and working.

— Didn't you call your family?

— I didn't contact my family for two months, until I was in very bad shape, because I didn't have enough money for food. I called and, of course, they told me to come home as soon as I could, there was no problem, they weren't going to have me sectioned again. They sent me money, because I was far away, and I ended up going back. A year went by and again they said, 'Paulo is crazy, he now wants to do theatre,' because my new passion, along with being a writer, was to do theatre. And they had me committed for a third time. And I escaped again, but this time they'd told the lift attendant not to let me escape. This time I escaped by taking advantage of a trip to the dentist, because the doctor in charge of my case came to the brilliant conclusion that it was a tooth that was about to come through that was making me so uncontrollable, because it was causing me pain. According to him, I didn't understand that the pain came from my tooth and that made me aggressive with everyone. On the way back from the dentist I escaped.

Once again I went off travelling and again returned to my family because I was completely broke and when I got back I said, 'Now I really am crazy,' because I was convinced by then that I wasn't sane and I didn't want to run away again. Two weeks went by and I was completely apathetic, not even reacting.

— *It couldn't have been easy on your family either.*

— The truth is that didn't even occur to me then. I was only thinking of myself. I only understood it later. But something paradoxical happened to me that was going to radically change my life. One day, I remember I was in my room, I had my desk, my bed, my clothes, all the things I loved. Well, I closed the door and said to myself, 'I can't go on living like this.' Because I'd lost my job at the newspaper, I'd lost my friends and had had to give up the theatre. So I thought that maybe my parents were right, maybe I was crazy. And for the first time I started acting really crazy: I closed the door to my bedroom and started destroying the whole room, my books that I loved so much, my collections of Sherlock Holmes, Henry Miller, my records, every remnant of my past. I tore it all to shreds. My parents heard me destroying everything and I wouldn't stop. So they went running to call the doctor who'd treated me in the asylum, but he wasn't in. They phoned another doctor, who I remember very well, because he was a man with no nose, a very curious character, a psychiatrist called Fajardo. When he arrived, he opened the door and confronted all that destruction. I thought they'd take me straight back to the asylum. But much to my surprise I heard him ask me calmly, smiling, 'What happened here?' 'Don't you see? I've wrecked everything,' I told him. And he, without batting an eye, answered, 'Well done! Now that you've torn everything to bits, you can start a new life. You've done exactly what you needed to do, no more, no less, you've destroyed a negative past in order to embark on a positive future.' 'But, what are you saying?' I answered, without recovering from the shock at hearing a psychiatrist tell me I'd done very well, destroying my entire room and all the things most dear to me. And he told me again, 'You've done the only thing you needed to do. Finish with the nightmare of the past. Now your life can start anew.'

— *How did your parents react?*

— They were very understanding and they agreed with what the strange psychiatrist had said. And they said, 'Now you're well you're going to start over from the beginning, it's over. Let's pick up everything you've broken and throw it all away.' Juan, that man saved me, because I'd reached the edge of real madness, and the worst was that I'd accepted it, resigned myself to it.

— *Did you keep in touch with that psychiatrist?*

— That day, when he was leaving, he told me, 'Now I'll guide the process.' I went to see him fifteen or twenty times until one day he said, 'You have to walk on your own two feet now. You're practically cured. You're a little crazy but we all are.' And that's when my rebelliousness erupted so strongly. I said to myself: it doesn't matter if I'm a little crazy, because we all need to confront our own madness, what I have to do now is live to the fullest, do everything I enjoy, deny myself nothing.

I'd lost everything: the newspaper, my friends, the theatre and even my girlfriend, who was very young and left me when they put me in the asylum, because she wasn't allowed in and I wasn't allowed out.

— Did you feel hatred or bitterness towards your parents for committing you to a mental hospital when you weren't crazy?

— No, never. They were convinced I hated them, but it wasn't true. They took me there out of love, a mistaken love, a desperate, dominating love, but when all's said and done, because they loved me. They didn't put me in an asylum because they hated me, but because they wanted to help me build my life. It was a desperate measure, crazy, which affected them more than it did me. But at the same time, that experience allowed me to realize the good fight, to confront myself.

— How did you react when you found out, not long ago, about the actual reasons your parents had you committed to the asylum?

— The only time I had a moment of hatred and bitterness was, in fact, a few weeks ago, when I read the report the asylum had written up about the causes of my being committed. I became furious because it was all so absurd, I couldn't even believe it. But the one who took the brunt of it was my English editor, against whom I vented my rage, who couldn't understand a thing. I was saying, 'How could anyone stand this shit-hole of a hotel!' And I phoned up to complain, because when I went to Dublin to sign books they put me on a television programme I didn't like. The person at the other end of the line said, 'But why are you being like this?'

Then we went to a park near the hotel and I calmed down. It was the only time I reacted angrily against the asylum incident. But I truly don't have any bitterness towards my parents over it. I promised not to talk about that painful experience while they were still alive and I'm only doing it now because my mother's not alive anymore and my father is very elderly, but entirely lucid, and he's followed the promotion of my novel, *Veronika Decides to Die*. I think talking about this story of mine was a relief to him. And he was even more pleased when, by way of the many letters I've received, he found out that he wasn't the only one to have done such a thing, since the same thing had happened in many families.

— Did your parents ever attempt to justify themselves to you?

— No, they never tried to justify themselves, but they did ask me to forgive them. They said, 'Forgive us, it was the greatest mistake of our lives,' but they never told me why they'd done it. But these things affect everybody, as Ortega y Gasset said, 'I am myself and my circumstances.' We all suffered, no doubt about it.

— Is that when you started your hippy phase?

— Yes. The hippy movement was my new family, my new tribe. I tried to go back to university, but it wasn't my thing anymore. And that's when I really got into the world of sex and drugs.

I started to think that maybe I was a homosexual because my mother thought I had sexual problems. And then I thought to get over my doubts I'd have to try it. And so I did. The first time I didn't like the experience at all, perhaps because I was extremely nervous. A year went by and I still had my doubts, so I made another attempt. That time I wasn't nervous, but I still didn't like it. And so I said to myself: third time lucky, I'll try one last time and if I'm still not attracted then I can't be a homosexual. And that didn't turn me on either. I was twenty-three then. My doubts came about when I was working in the theatre and there are a lot of homosexuals in that world, maybe I was one without knowing it. And so, I finally got over my doubts.

— *Freed from that concern, you began to work and travel once more. You were in the prime of youth. How do you remember it?*

— Yes, I started giving classes for passing the entrance exam to the theatre school. I made enough money to live for the whole year. I did children's theatre as well. It was seasonal work, three months of work and then nine months free to travel, which was very cheap back then. I remember I crossed the United States not speaking English and went as far as Mexico on two hundred dollars; it was crazy but in the United States you could by a ticket for a month and a half's travel for ninety-nine dollars. I didn't have enough money to pay for a place to sleep, so I slept on the bus for eight hours and then I'd wake up somewhere, not knowing where, but it didn't matter.

I was always with a group, because in those days there was a lot of solidarity among hippies. We would take night bus rides so we could sleep in the Greyhound and that way we saw a lot of places. From then on I started to get totally absorbed in hippy culture.

– And what happened to your passion for writing?

– I didn't get any writing done then, but when I got back to Brazil a phenomenon had begun called the *underground*, an alternative press. It was during the dictatorship, but it wasn't a left-wing press, it was more for those who were looking for an alternative that didn't fit in with the established system, the Beatles, the Rolling Stones, Peter Fonda with the American flag and *Easy Rider*. It was classic American pop culture. I had a girlfriend – women have always played a very important role in my life – who had an apartment, but we didn't have any money. One day we started to look for work. We found a company that had a rotary press; I started up a new magazine that only ever had two issues, but which was instrumental in my future work. A record producer from CBS, the same age as me, got to know of me through the first issue of the magazine; he was called Raúl Seixas, and he later became a great singer.

— In some circles you're still known as the author of Raúl Seixas' famous songs.

— He got in touch with me and asked why I didn't write song lyrics, but Raúl came from within the system, he was a producer and we had a lot of prejudice against those within the system, because our philosophy was to go against everything that was established and secure. I'm well acquainted with prejudice. I then adopted a totally impartial attitude because I recognized both sides of the argument.

He produced Jerry Adriani, this Julio Iglesias-style bolero singer I hated. I said to myself, 'But that guy's awful!' And nevertheless, in the end, in spite of my prejudices, he turned out to be a charming person, fantastic, marvellous. There was a stupendous project called, *Poet, Show Your Face*, with all the lyricists of Brazilian music. My producer asked me who I wanted to sing my lyrics and I said, 'Adriani, he deserves it,' and it turned out fantastic.

— How many lyrics did you write for Raúl Seixas?

— Sixty-five. By then we had a salary, we'd started with the alternative press thing. Adriani was very moved that I chose him to sing my lyrics and it was a way not to pay him, because these things have no price, but to pay homage his importance to Raúl and to me.

— And you began to get out of your financial difficulties?

– Of course. Imagine, for the first time in my life I became rich overnight. I went to the bank to see how much I had in my account and found a deposit of almost forty-thousand dollars. I didn't have enough money to go to the movies or eat out and the next day I had forty-thousand dollars. It was madness! The first thing I thought was to buy myself a racing car, but I ended up buying a flat.

My parents, due to that strange association people make between money and success, started to spoil me. I was twenty-three and my father helped me buy a flat. He lent me another thirty-thousand dollars, which I soon paid back, since I kept earning lots of money. By 1978 I owned five apartments. I was thirty years old. These are the key people, who sometimes, like omens, appear in your life and change it for you, just as had already happened to me with Fajardo, the psychiatrist, and later with another person when I got out of prison. It's odd that it's not usually institutions but people who shape the direction of your life, for better or for worse.

– *You were also imprisoned for political reasons; you were kidnapped and tortured, weren't you?*

– Three times. Everything happens to me three times. In *The Alchemist* there's a proverb that says: 'Everything that happens once can never happen again. But everything that happens twice, will surely happen a third time.' Many times I see things this way, they're symbols, signs I experienced in my life. In reality, I was imprisoned six times, three in the mental hospital and three in prison.

— Which was worse?

— Prison was a thousand times worse. It was the worst experience of my life, because along with what happened inside, when I got out I was a leper. Everyone said, 'Don't go near him, he's been in prison, there must have been a reason for it.'

Prison is the embodiment of hatred, cruelty, fatal power and total impotence. The first time they took me, I was with a gang of kids in Paraná and there was a bank robbery. Having long hair and no ID, I was grabbed straight away and taken in. They held me for a week and that time they didn't do anything to me.

— And the other times?

— Those were more serious and unexpected, because I was working with Raúl by then. I was very well-known for my songs and was making a lot of money. I was also already involved in magic, and I felt almost omnipotent, but nevertheless I ended up back in jail.

— Why did they arrest you?

– I remember it as if it were yesterday. I felt immensely stupid because, having got where I was, we started to believe in the idea of an alternative society, and Raúl and I had a sort of utopia. We went to Brasilia to do a concert and I said a few words about our ideas on society and our aspirations to change things. It seemed totally innocent to me. We were just two young idealists. But the next day Raúl received a piece of paper saying he had to report to the police. He went, and I went with him, and I sat down in the waiting room. Raúl came out singing a song I can't remember now, but with different lyrics and in English. He went to make a telephone call and said to me, 'Their problem's with you, not me.' Then I understood what he meant by the song, and when I went to get up they said, 'Where do you think you're going?' 'For a coffee,' I told them. 'No, no, ask your friend to bring you one,' they answered. And I didn't get to leave there. Although that time wasn't that serious either, because I had a romantic idea of jail, I thought being in prison for political reasons was part of the adventure we were undertaking.

– *Did your parents help you out?*

– Yes. They got me a lawyer, who told me to calm down, that even though I was in jail those horrors you heard about the dictatorship's tortures weren't going to happen to me. It was close to the end of the worst phase of the military government and

General Geisel had decided to initiate a period of liberalization. There was the hard line, the extreme right, who had a huge war machine in place, which they'd used to finish off the guerrillas, and now had to justify their existence. They knew I was one of those crazy alternative society people, who had nothing to do with guerrillas, but they had almost no political prisoners since they'd killed almost all of them and they had to look for new enemies to justify themselves.

After the lawyer came, they let me leave and I signed a document saying the government had no responsibility for anything and other stupid things like that.

— But then the worst happened.

— Yes, as soon as I got out a group of paramilitaries kidnapped my wife and me. We were in a taxi. I showed them the paper I'd signed in prison and they said, 'So, it's true you're a guerrilla, since you haven't even gone home.' And they added that I had gone underground with my guerrilla comrades.

I was disappeared. They were the worst days of my life. And this time my parents couldn't help me, since they didn't know where I was.

— Where had they taken you?

– I don't know. I discussed it with a few people after I got out, and we think – because no one knows, since the first thing they do is put a hood over your head so you won't see anything – that I was in Barao de Mezquita Street, where there was a military barracks infamous as a torture centre, but it's just a guess. I was always blindfolded or completely alone, there was never anyone with me when I could see. In this case, the State wasn't responsible either, because I wasn't in prison; I was with the paramilitaries, according to them, and the great fear was that I could be transferred to São Paulo, where the worst of the repression took place. I talked many times about this with Fray Betto, because those moments for me were a horror, and he told me, 'the horror is always the first days'. And that's how it was for me.

– *Were you and your wife held captive for a long time?*

– I was held for a week, but you can't measure that sort of thing in days, it feels like years, because you're totally lost, impotent, you don't know where you are, you don't have anyone to talk to. The only person whose face I saw was the photographer, because he had to take the hood off to take the photo. And the torture …

(Paulo Coelho did not want to go into detail about that week of torture because talking about it would involve reliving one of the most painful and humiliating experiences of his life. But they always tortured him with the hood on. And years later he had the feeling he clearly recognized the voice of one of his torturers and that the torturer had also recognized his victim.)

– *What did they want from you?*

– For me to talk, to tell them about guerrilla activity in Bahía. I didn't know a thing, I had no idea. The technique was the following: if the guy's guilty, he has to speak quickly, because after a while you get used to the tortures. At the beginning, between the kidnapping and the torture, you don't react. I remember they got me and my then wife out of the taxi, they kidnapped both of us, I saw the Gloria Hotel and their guns, everything really fast. 'Get out!' they said to my wife and grabbed her by the hair and pulled her out. I looked at the hotel and thought, 'I'm going to die now.' I said to myself, 'How stupid to die looking at a hotel!' These are the stupid things that occur to you at the most tragic moments. They put her in one car and me in another; it was much worse for her because they told her they were going to kill her, they didn't tell me that. They grabbed me, put a hood over my head and told me they weren't going to kill me, to keep calm, but how was I supposed to be calm when I knew they were going to put me in a concentration camp and torture me from head to toe! And I couldn't tell them anything, even if I'd wanted to, because I didn't know a thing about the guerrillas.

(At this point in the conversation, Coelho wanted to tell something very intimate that still torments him to this day. One of the times they took him hooded to relieve himself, his wife was in the next cubicle. She recognized his voice and asked him, 'If you're Paulo, speak to me, please.' He had a moment of panic and though he certainly recognized his wife's voice, he didn't dare answer her. That's how he found out that his wife was also in the prison and was surely being tortured as he was. But he didn't have the courage to say a single word to her and went back to his cell. Coelho, his eyes moist, told me, 'It was the most cowardly day of my life, which I'll regret as long as I live.' That woman, when they both got out of the torture chambers, asked him just one favour: that he never again pronounce her name. And Coelho has kept that promise. Whenever he mentions her he says: 'my wife who shall be nameless.'

CHAPTER III

Private Life

❦

*'I was never terrified of death because I saw it
up close so many times.'*

*'The last thing I wanted, when I became a
celebrity, was to lose my friends.'*

❦

Many of Coelho's readers will wonder what his private life is like, how one of the world's most widely-read writers behaves behind closed doors. What are his fears, his small satisfactions, his worries? Those lucky enough to know the man well, might point out that such a celebrity doesn't really exist, because Paulo Coelho – despite his fame, the millions of dollars his work earns him, the international demand for his presence – is a totally approachable, available, generous, simple person, almost childlike at times. A person who doesn't hide the black spots of his past and who enthusiastically enjoys what he does and the positive reception that greets his books, especially from young people. He tends to forget the negative reactions as quickly as he hears them. He considers envy to be the greatest sin as well as the stupidest. A saint? No. Coelho is a character with great passions, great defects, sometimes with great genius, with his small burden of vanity, capable of being very tough when he wants to be. But, at the same time, he possesses a great capacity for dedication and a sincere desire to help others find their personal destiny. That is what has saved him from a difficult, sometimes tragic past and it is that which has taken him more than once to the edge of madness and death.

– *How do you conduct your private life? Do you protect it?*

– No, I don't protect it, but let's define what exactly my private life is.

— What is outside your public life, your intimacy.

— When I'm in Brazil, I am basically a very solitary being, not because I protect this private life, nor because I have anything to hide — although I do have, like anyone — but what I have to hide I do in the most open way possible, which is the best way to hide something. I do it so much in the light of day that people don't believe it and say, 'It can't be.' But that's the way it is.

— Do you consider yourself a sociable man?

— No. I'm really quite unsociable, although I also want variety. I love my work, I am an enthusiast of what I do. If I have to travel, I travel; if I have to do the hardest thing for me — giving speeches — I give speeches. As for interviews, I find them easier, because they're simply conversations, but I dread speeches.

— And so much travelling. You spend more than half the year roaming around the world.

— It's true I spend more time outside Brazil than I do at home now that, as you know, publishers want authors to promote their books. The truth is I take the trips, hotels, airports, and all that, if not agreeably then stoically, in the sense that I don't let it bother me, it's part of my philosophy. Encountering so many of my readers helps me, taking the pulse, sharing my hopes and ideas with them. In those meetings with people there are some very emotional moments. I like it. It's enriching. And also you meet interesting people when you travel – people who become important to your life. You and I, for example, met thanks to one of my trips to Madrid, for the launch of *The Fifth Mountain*, as you'll recall.

– You don't mind travelling despite your fear of aeroplanes?

– No, I'm not afraid anymore, I used to be. I got over it in the city of Ávila, the city of Saint Theresa of Jesus, the great Spanish mystic. I had an intense religious experience, and most of my fears were left behind once and for all, among them my fear of flying. Speaking of aeroplanes, I'll never forget a trip I once took when I was still afraid. Sitting beside me was a woman who did nothing but drink. Looking at me, she said, 'Don't think I'm an alcoholic, it's just that I'm scared to death.' And she proceeded to tell me everything that could happen to us if the aeroplane had a fault, if it crashed. In all the gory details, as if we were living through it. Some of the experience of fright is in *The Fifth Mountain*, which also touches on this theme.

– So, you're a fearless man?

— No, I still have lots of little fears, like speaking in public, for example.

— *What about the fear of death?*

— No, I'm not afraid of death, because I've already faced it many times in my life. There were times when I was involved in drugs and black magic, as I'll tell you, when I was convinced I was going to die.

The truth is, thinking about it now, I don't think a fear of death or how I'd die have been constant in my life. For example, the fear I had of aeroplanes wasn't so much a fear of dying but a fear of always being in a state of flux, a little lost.

— *When did you lose your fear of death?*

— In reality, I lost my fear of death when I made the pilgrimage to Santiago. I had a very interesting and important experience in which I lived through my own death. Since that moment I've never felt afraid of death. I now see death as something that instils in me a strong will to live. Castaneda spoke very well on death and wasn't afraid of it either.

— *But death will arrive one day, as to us all. How do you imagine it now?*

– In *The Pilgrimage* I describe death as a kind of angel, a tranquil figure I feel always at my side. Of course, I'm fully aware I have to die. That's why I don't invest to accumulate riches, I invest in life itself. And I believe it to be what is missing in our civilization. Only when we have full consciousness of the fact that we will die do we feel one hundred per cent alive.

– *You're not afraid of death, what about failure?*

– For me, it's very difficult now to conceive of failure. Whatever happens in the future, it's unlikely I'll think of myself as a failure, because I've achieved much more in life than I ever hoped or dreamt. So, not failure, but I could possibly be defeated. And in that case, I'd lick my wounds and start over again.

– *What you do fear is that, after your death, things you hadn't wanted to publish in your lifetime will be published.*

– Yes, and I've been very emphatic about that in my will, in which I leave all my assets to the foundation I told you about. I've also stated in my will that I do not want, under any circumstance, anyone to publish anything I did not authorize when alive. Although this would be very difficult, because each time I write something and then decide not to publish it, I destroy it in order to avoid this danger that has befallen so many other writers, and which I find so disagreeable. It strikes me as indecent that things writers did not wish to publish when living should come to light after their deaths. Except in cases in which they themselves have said that certain things should not be published until after their deaths.

— *Do you believe in reincarnation?*

— What really calms me is not thinking of a possible reincarnation, but rather being alive. I keep death very close and it's as if she's sitting in front of me to remind me each minute, 'Pay attention, do what you do well, don't leave until tomorrow what you could do today, don't entertain feelings of guilt, don't loathe yourself.' Death is the most natural thing that can happen to us.

— *And faced with fear, how do you act?*

— If I have to tell you the truth, Juan, I've always been scared of lots of things, but one of my qualities has always been to confront danger bravely. I've never been intimidated by anything. Fear has never in my life paralysed me.

— *Do you overcome it or suffer it?*

– I never get over fear, but I face it down. To overcome it would be to conquer it, but I don't conquer it, I keep it, I live with it, without it paralysing me. I keep going. Courage is fear saying its prayers.

– *Returning to your private life, what makes you most uncomfortable in social relations?*

– The most complicated part for me is the cocktail parties which I have to attend. When they're with booksellers, I'm fine, but when there's some important person that someone's promised to intro- duce me to, and I can't say no because this person's helped me a lot, I endure it very badly. It doesn't suit me to play at celebrity. I have to go to these functions – sometimes I end up enjoying myself – but I assure you that, if possible, I avoid them. I prefer to stay quietly in the hotel, reading or whatever.

– *And when you're here at home, in Brazil?*

– When I'm travelling I'm in a state of constant expansion, of con- stant fluidity, so it's as if all that energy comes back to me again when I get home. Now my new book, *Veronika Decides to Die*, has come out and I'll have to start travelling again, but if not, I'd stay at home all day quite happily. Today, for example, I was invited to a wedding, but people know how I am – I send presents but I don't go out – I love being here, with my computer, or walking along the beach.

– Are you good at being alone?

– I am good at being alone. But then I am never really completely alone, because I'm always with Cristina, my wife, but she stays in her *atelier*, here opposite, and I stay in front of my computer. We spend hours without exchanging a word, but we sense each other's presence. What I love is to go out for a walk along Copacabana beach. For me, this walk, after getting out of bed late, since I work at night, is a ritual I can't give up. I like walking, meeting people and doing things in the simplest possible way.

– It can't be easy for you to do things simply now that to many you've become an unapproachable person.

– Yes, the only problem fame has caused me is something very strange: that people start saying something to you that for me isn't true, and I think in ninety per cent of other people who become famous it mustn't be either. People start saying to you, 'I know you're very busy …' and it's not true, I'm not very busy. 'You don't have any time left for anything or anybody,' and it's not true. Look, today I got up at noon because I wanted to see France's match, then I had a long interview, slept for a bit … but I don't have anything to do. What am I going to do? Well, maybe write some newspaper columns in advance because I know I've got a heavy workload coming up, but since I returned to Brazil from my travels I haven't done anything.

— *But that's something that occurs inevitably with all famous people. People think they're unreal beings, without time even to breathe.*

— It even creates a barrier between you and your old friends. Even your closest friends start treating you more formally, thinking that something's changed about you, that you're not the one they used to know and they start to treat you differently as well. Often you hear these friends say, 'I liked that Paulo when he wasn't well-known.' But, how can they say that, when I'm the same? On the contrary, now I'm happier with my old friends, since they're my friends not because I'm famous, but because they were before, when I was nobody.

— *But the reality is that when someone becomes a celebrity it's difficult not to be seen as one, even by old friends.*

— Yes, but I still exist, and the basis of my exterior stability is my friendships. If I lose contact with my friends, I lose everything, I lose my balance. That already happened to me in the past, I committed that error when I wrote song lyrics. I believed I was king of the world, I started to get famous, to earn money, I worked for an international record company and the first thing I did was change friends. I said to myself, 'Now I'm very important and I haven't got anything in common with these hippies with their alternative ideas.' And what happened? Well, the day I lost that job I was left completely alone, because the people I thought were my new friends stopped calling and I'd already lost my other friends. I learned by that experience and I said, 'If I get another chance, I'm going to keep my friends, no matter the cost.'

– Have you managed it this time?

– Not entirely, but this time through no fault of my own, since my sincere desire was not to lose my friends despite the fame that might surround me. But it's not easy, because they're the ones who start treating me more formally. At the beginning, when something came out in the paper about me, they'd all phone me to tell me they'd read it or seen me on television. Now, I talk to the Pope and there's not a single call to say, 'I saw you with the Pope …'

– Is it envy?

– No, I don't think it's envy, it's more because they think I'm unapproachable, that a person who's been received by the Pope can't keep up his old friendships anymore. But they're wrong.

— *Maybe they think, now that you're famous, it's normal for the Pope to receive you.*

— It could be, but I don't. I try to maintain the same childish view, that's what drives me to keep going forward. If I lose that, I lose enthusiasm. That's why I like meeting the ordinary readers I cross paths with on my tours of the Brazilian interior. Brazil is a fantastic country. And the people, especially the people of the interior, are very worthy, open, not easily intimidated. They're sincere and unaffected, while I notice that success often slightly intimidates people close to you. Because of that, in the end you find yourself with just a handful of friends who don't allow themselves to be intimidated, who might also have the same problems as you. They understand you and don't keep their distance.

— *For the rest, you're no longer just one person, you're two: you and your celebrity. It could be that, on the one hand, you are the unapproachable celebrity and, on the other, the person you used to be, but they think he's gone now, that you've become the celebrity irremediably.*

— But I never left myself, like I did in 1979–80, as far as I know. Today, as you know, I am approachable, I'm accessible, or I'm unapproachable about things that don't interest me, but not in life. But as I lose old friends I'm making new ones. Perhaps they're not the ones who once climbed a mountain with me, but all the same they're good friends you can count on.

— How do you defend yourself against the inevitable envy your success must provoke, especially among other writers?

— I protect myself against envy with magic spells. I create a protective barrier so I don't have to struggle against it. To my mind, envy is the most destructive of the cardinal sins. Because the envious don't say, 'I want to achieve that.' No, what they say is, 'I don't want so-and-so to have that.' That's very mean, the person levels the world from below. I know I can destroy myself, that God can destroy me, but not envy. It only destroys the one who takes it to their breast like a venomous snake.

CHAPTER IV

Politics and Ethics

⋈

'To me, politics is about breaking down the
wall of cultural conventions that surrounds us.'

'We have to make it understood that a writer
is no more important than someone who sells coconuts.'

⋈

During his whole agitated youth, Paulo Coelho was an activist in the most progressive movements; even the Beatles struck him as conservative. He was always radical. He dreamt of an alternative society and explored Marxism. In his political and ethical undertakings, he has always shown himself to be a radical confronting the system. He paid a high price: mental hospital, prison and torture.

Now that he's a successful man, famous the world over, his attention vied for by the world's great and good, adored by his readers, where does he situate himself politically and ethically? He continues to consider himself a political animal, but at the same time, wants to keep away from any partisan temptation. Deep down, as in his youth, he is still a romantic who wants to believe that a strong spiritual conviction, a love of mystery, tolerance, and that part of positive magic that exists hidden in each life, could afford us a less unhappy, less cruel world, full of realizable dreams. Amidst a world rampant with violence and insatiable yearnings for power, he believes that we mustn't dispense with the fragile child we all carry within which speaks of lost innocence, which we mustn't renounce if we want to understand something of what we are and why we live.

— *You live here in Brazil, although you spend half the year travelling the world. This developing country, rich in potential, still has forty million poor people who live at the margin of the system, totally abandoned to their fate. Beside them we are all rich. You lacked for many things before reaching your celebrated status. Now you're a rich man, who earns millions of dollars and lives in a magnificent house in Río de Janeiro, facing this dream world, Copacabana beach ... I'm sure many of your readers would like to know where you situate yourself politically and ethically before the challenges of the Third World.*

– Obviously my vision of the world and politics has changed over the years. I've lived through the most radical experiences, as you well know. I have seen the positive and the negative in each. We are all in some way orphans of our dreams for the fairer society we fought and paid for in flesh.

I am now convinced that it's not the great ideologies that will change the world. Many of them have failed and the birth of new and even more dangerous ones remains a threat, such as the new fundamentalisms. I still feel myself to be a political animal, but the politics contained in my books concern breaking down the walls of cultural conventions that lead to fanaticism. I believe the most important thing, as the Spanish philosopher Fernando Savater affirms, is a strong ethical commitment from each one of us, without which future society will be ever more fratricidal and ever less fraternal.

– And along that line, what is your personal undertaking?

– I am convinced that each person must now make their contribution to society. Because of that I believe strongly in the new wave of solidarity that is growing around the world, especially among young people.

In order not to remain in the ethereal world of good intentions, I wanted to do something concrete, within my possibilities, in the field of solidarity, and I have created a foundation in my name that will live on after my death.

—*Exactly what does it consist of?*

— In the first place, I'll tell you that my wife, Cristina, is in charge of it. She keeps watch over it so that the aims and objects we've set are complied with to the letter. From the beginning I've wanted it to be serious and transparent. It has five objectives: the abandoned children of Brazil; poor and needy elderly people, the translation into other languages of classic Brazilian authors, to allow the very rich culture of my country to become better known. I'm mainly interested in classics by deceased authors, in order to avoid the problems of jealousy and useless vanity. The fourth objective is the study of Brazil's prehistory, the unwritten history of this country I love so much. We're looking at ways to release gradually the results of our research. I've already been in touch with the Ministry of Culture. And I've also thought about publishing the results on the Internet. And, lastly, the fifth objective is the only one which will disappear with my death, for it's something very personal: I have proposed to help certain people realize their life's dream or heart's desire. Naturally, I get asked for everything. But I alone decide who to help – it could be giving someone a guitar or a collection of books to a bibliophile, or defraying someone's costs so they can make the pilgrimage to Santiago, an experience that changed my life.

— They'll be hounding you from all corners of the globe.

— They already are. Each day, a large part of the bundle of post I receive is asking for something. And I won't deny that whether I agree or not depends to a great extent on whether or not I'm in a bad mood. I let myself be guided by my instincts there. I alone decide. The rest is under the direction of the foundation.

— How much money do you dedicate to the foundation? Because I've read different, contradictory sums?

— Well, let's get this cleared up. I allocate three hundred thousand dollars a year to the foundation out of my author's royalties. But last year, due to an error of mine in an interview, it became four hundred thousand dollars. Since I'd said it, so as not to be a liar, we spent another hundred thousand dollars on a new house for the street children from the *favelas*, because the one we had was too small. I'm afraid my mistake is going to cost me an extra hundred thousand dollars every year from now on.

— Why have you decided to give publicity to the foundation? At the beginning no one knew anything about it. You didn't speak about your work.

— That's true, but one day a little item came out in a newspaper and to my surprise, thanks to that, I came face to face with the impressive network of silent solidarity that exists within society. It's quite disarming, because you think maybe humanity's not so bad after all. Thousands of people offered to help us.

I also discovered that this network is extremely varied, because these are not just idealistic, impecunious young people or adults who want to do something for others, but also important businessmen, even captains of industry with lots of money. But where there isn't any difference is in the enthusiasm they put into doing something concrete for people more needy than themselves. And without a big song and dance, on tiptoes, not letting the right hand know what the left hand's doing, as the Bible says.

— And where do you place yourself in the more strictly political sphere?

— As I told you before, I consider myself a political man but not a party man. I think my books are political, because I help people realize many things with my personal legend, with the awakening of the feminine side, the need to tear up the official 'Manual of Good Conduct' and pay the price for their dreams. As well as alerting people to all kinds of fanaticism, to those who try to take over the role of other's consciences, to the false culture of knowledge and to the hypocrisy of certain politicians who, instead of serving the citizens, are self-serving, using citizens to satisfy their personal whims.

– Have you ever been tempted by party politics, given your fame?

– Stand for election? No. I'm not interested in party politics. But what I do is political. Is it not political to attempt to destroy the wall that separates the people from power, the fusion between the imaginary and the real? Traditional politics already has its leaders and popular representatives. I'm interested in another kind of politics.

– You've often been heard to affirm that doing things well and enthusiastically is also political.

– Yes. For me, one way of participating in politics is by repeating in every possible way that it is necessary to live life with enthusiasm, that each of us is responsible for our own fate and can't delegate it to anyone, that a writer, no matter how famous, is no more important to the world than someone who sells coconuts, or a policeman who watches over our safety in the streets, although sometimes he may erroneously feel himself to be more important than anybody.

For me, politics is contributing to changing what I call the 'Academy', that is the fossilized, bureaucratic, conventional wisdom that thinks itself the only repository of knowledge. The power of the privileged. We have to go back to giving free rein to creativity, giving the common man a voice, considering that there shouldn't be an educated elite who think they're privileged with titles and honours to impose their culture on the rest.

In this sense, I believe the Internet can help substantially. It is an instrument that, despite all the dangers it brings with it, can contribute to everyone having the possibility of getting their voice heard. If the powerful do not destroy the Internet by taking control of it, I think it could become a formidable forum for universal debate, where no one feels excluded. I believe it could create a sane anarchy, that can't be controlled by those who hold world power. But maybe that's just another utopia I want to believe in.

— But if someone asked you where you stood on the new Third World liberation movements, like the Zapatistas in Chiapas[3] or the Landless Movement[4] in Brazil, how would you answer?

[3] Guerrilla movement in Mexico, demanding land and rights for Mexico's Mayan peasants. In 1994, the Zapatistas took over four towns in the region of Chiapas, the poorest state in Mexico, to protest against a government and a social order which they felt offered nothing to the indigenous people.
[4] Peasant movement fighting against the large landowners and struggling to attain their own property.

– I always take a position. I never refuse to give my opinion, in favour or against, but I never keep quiet, I never keep out of it.

– *So, what's your opinion on these movements?*

– It depends. I see Chiapas more romantically, because I don't know that much about it. As for the Landless Movement, which I am closer to, I admit there are moments when I'm not so much in agreement with them, because it seems to me they don't always act coherently.

(The next day Coelho wanted to return to the subject. He feared he may have been unclear and he was concerned readers would be unsure of his position.)

– *You said you never refuse to give your opinion on controversial political issues, that you didn't mind showing your face.*

– That's true, but there's another problem. Look, ever since I became famous, everyone wants my opinion on the most extraordinary subjects, from the death of Princess Diana to football. Okay on the latter, because I'm a big fan and know something about it, but there are things I have no idea about and they oblige me to give an opinion. Something similar happens with politics. I don't consider myself a man removed from politics, since politics arranges our lives. You can't be politically neutral because otherwise you're letting others decide about your life and interests. You have to participate actively. But I'm not a professional politician, nor an expert in political philosophy.

— But, for example, with the Landless Movement it is not difficult to have an opinion. We have a lot of information, it's more a matter of seeing where your heart lies.

— It's more than just a matter for the heart. You have to know how to reflect on the phenomenon. That movement started off really well, it seems to me, with very concrete actions, since there are these enormous estates and it is logical that landless people would think of occupying those properties and creating a new social situation. A short time ago I was interviewed on the issue and my position was very clear.

What's happening is that, perhaps due to the movement's lack of experience, things I am less happy with are happening. There are, for example, unjustifiable occupations. At the end of last year I met Stedile, the leader of the movement, at a dinner at the house of the UNESCO representative in Brasilia.

— What was your impression?

– We had a conversation and exchanged opinions. He struck me as a person with his head screwed on straight, but I don't believe he's using his huge political power in an entirely adequate way. And I'm referring to conventional politics. My fear is that he could be manipulated by right-wing forces, as happened to the Brazilian guerrillas. After a certain point, because of certain mistakes they'd made, they added fuel to the fire and gave justification to the right for their repression. That is also my fear today. I believe they've taken some things too far and this saddens and worries me, because they could put the struggle of a democratic left in jeopardy.

– *You see nothing positive in this movement?*

– Of course I do, that's why it saddens me that because of these errors they could be used. One of the most positive things I see is that they seem to be starting to form alliances with other forces. It is always necessary to balance the rigour of ideologies with compassion, to know how to make sense of the times we're living through. On the other hand, I see the PT (left-wing *Partido de Trabajadores*, or Workers' Party, led by Lula) as much more mature. The Landless Movement can be a positive force for the PT, but it could also be negative if they lose sight of the art of the possible in politics.

— How do you view the situation in general in Brazil, an emerging country with many problems but that could become a reference point for all of Latin America, if it achieves a social reform that invites the poorest to the table?

— In all sincerity, I'll tell you — I, who have never in my life been on the right — that the government we now have in power in Brazil is conscious of social issues. The president, Fernando Enrique Cardoso, has been in prison; we are not ashamed to say he's our President, as has happened on other occasions. He has been an important sociologist, he knows the political game, he has great international prestige and knows how to negotiate with everyone, an important thing in politics if you consider it to be the art of negotiation and compromise.

— In the last century there have been too many wars and too much blood spilt. We know nothing spectacular is going to happen in this new century, as you've already said very well. But we are faced, as Saramago says in my book, with the end of a civilization. And we're not able to sense what the one now being born will be like. How do you feel watching this civilization end? Afraid or hopeful?

— It's difficult to predict the future. What I can tell you is that it all depends on what happens in the next fifty years. They have marked the new millennium. A lot depends on whether people decide to set out on a serious, solid spiritual quest. Malraux already said that either this century will be spiritual or it won't.

Others say it will be the feminine century. On the contrary, the danger exists that the bomb of fundamentalism could explode. Paradoxically, to my understanding, fundamentalism implies a lack of faith.

— And what might be the antidote to the new wave of fundamentalism that is beginning to surround us?

— This might sound banal, but it's necessary to understand that our spiritual path must be a search for individual responsibility, not delegating it to masters or captains. It is necessary to increase the values of tolerance, the idea that there is space for everyone in every sector — in religion, politics and culture. No one should impose their world-view. As Jesus said, 'In my Father's house are many mansions.' There's no reason we should all have to live on the same floor or with the same ideas. Wealth lies in plurality, in diversity. The rest is fascism. With fundamentalism we would return to the deepest of the worst of the obscurantism of the past.

What has to be said is that one can be atheist or Muslim or Catholic or Buddhist or agnostic and it doesn't matter. Each person is responsible for their own conscience. The opposite irremediably leads to war, because it conceives of someone different as an enemy.

— Did you speak to the world's great economic gurus in Davos about the dangers of spiritual globalization?

– In Davos I was surprised to find that those who hold economic and political power right now are also interested in the themes of the new spirituality. They're not allied to fundamentalism but to spiritual freedom. I was very impressed, for example, by Shimon Peres, who explained to me his idea of how to achieve peace in the Middle East. He told me it was necessary to 'privatize' peace, that is, internalize it, meaning that we have to start with each and every person falling in love with peace and making it their life's work. That implies giving priority to tolerance over intolerance. And it's important this idea should come from Israel.

– *What is it you most fear in this century of 'globalization'?*

– I worry about the idea of economic globalization being carried over to the globalization of God. In the same way that the idea of a homogeneous culture made to everyone's measure horrifies me, I'm frightened of the idea of a standard God, dogmatically valid for everyone, as opposed to the personal, to what can be discovered by the colour of the consciousness of each human being. Culture and religion have to be the expression of the individual soul. The same community of believers has to be made up of free, original, different people, each with their own spiritual wealth. The great danger of the global market lies in producing a culture as universal mind-control. From there to a new Nazism, it's just a small step.

— You often mention the struggle, battles, the 'warrior of the light' subject of one of your books. Someone could think the warrior of light is closer to a warrior of peace. What is distinctive about the true warrior of light?

— Very simple. On the personal plane, accepting oneself as a person who cannot be polarized by fears, who struggles against them, and carries on in search of the personal legend. On the collective plane, by avoiding all forms of cultural, political or religious fundamentalism, avoiding everything that could be taken as exclusion of others, of those who are different, and by opening oneself enthusiastically to all new experiences: communication among men, co-participation and, if you'll allow me — although this word is much prostituted — love.

— On one occasion, I believe in Italy, you spoke of the 'ethic of risk'. How do you define it?

— For me, the ethic of risk involves the capacity to continue to be daring, despite the fact that everything around us screams for immobility. In fact, society imposes ever more strictures on our behaviour. The courage to infringe these rules is precisely the risk of true knowledge, which always implies the rupture of traditional, obsolete paradigms. Here lies the wisdom of the mad, which is the theme of my last novel, as you know.

— Are you one of those who believe that the new technologies and latest scientific advances are, in fact, rather negative for the development of the spirit?

— No. It is true that many people think technology has destroyed everything, that it has taken away our humanity. I don't believe it, and it's one of the few things I disagreed with when Saramago admitted his fear of these technologies in your book.

— Not exactly fear, he says they're not for his generation, that he has arrived too late, although it's true he does say that an e-mail 'can never be stained by a tear'.

— What I want to say is that technology and scientific advancement, from the Internet to mobile phones and all the rest of the new things that might rain down on us, make up part of humanity's path to make our work easier and more comfortable. The important thing is not to turn them into gods, but to know how to use them for what they are — tools to make our lives easier and give us greater power to communicate with like-minded people. Because don't forget, humanity's greatest sin is non-communication, unwanted and unloved solitude, forgetting that we were created to find each other, to be each other's mirrors. And everything that makes it easier to find each other and communicate, definitely contributes to our becoming less inhuman and more sympathetic.

CHAPTER V

The Feminine

✣

'All my life has been governed by
feminine energy, by women.'

'Before coming to know the feminine
I didn't know the meaning of compassion.'

✣

It is impossible to know Paulo Coelho without understanding the part played in his life and work by the feminine element. As he admits in these conversations, women have occupied and continue to occupy a fundamental space in his life. He, who has for the most part trodden the path of the warrior of light, of the struggle, in sympathy with his masculine identity, decided one day to discover the woman who is also within him. And that was when he met a new element of his life head on: compassion, letting himself be carried away by life without always having to defend himself. It was also when he discovered the feminine part of God. His books cannot now be understood without that vision he has of woman and what she represents within and outside of us. Two of his books: *Brida* and *Veronika Decides to Die* have women's names in the title, and in many others the female characters are fundamental. But perhaps the work that best reveals his feminine side is *By the River Piedra I Sat Down and Wept*, which Coelho wrote from the point of view of a woman.

– Let's talk about the part of you that is feminine, because I am convinced that this century is fundamentally going to be a century of women.

– I, too, am sure that this century will be affected by the greater presence of women in society. Man is finishing this century with a larger identity crisis than woman, who, at least, knows better what she wants and the autonomy she lacks in order to get it, after centuries of absolute masculine domination.

As far as I'm concerned, we can talk about two things: about the women in my life and about the woman who I am, since I feel myself to be man and woman at the same time.

— Let's start with what women have meant to you in your life.

— The truth is my whole life has been ruled, in some way, by feminine energy, by women. We're in total confessional mode here, so I'm going to tell you something very personal, very emblematic of my relationship with women, because what happened to me with my first love is what has happened later with all the women I have met in my life, including my current wife, Cristina.

I very much wanted to work in the theatre. It was, as I've said, my first dream, along with being a writer. But I didn't have a penny, because I wasn't earning any money. I was also wrapped up in problems with my family, who couldn't stand my artistic capriciousness and expected me to follow a more respectable profession, like being a lawyer or something like that. This was when they had me committed to a mental hospital. I was the black sheep of the family, but as a good warrior, I kept fighting for my dream of working in the theatre.

— And a woman became your guardian angel?

– Yes, and it was one of the most difficult times for me, although now I realize I was forging my resolve with all those tests. If I can live at peace now, without interior conflicts, I owe it all to those battles with my parents, which could have destroyed me forever, but, thanks to God, helped to temper my spirit for future struggles ...

Anyway, at that time, I was still hoping to work in the theatre, but I didn't know who to approach, when a woman, almost a girl, came into my life. I was eighteen and she was seventeen. She was emblematic in my life.

– *In what sense?*

– I'm going to tell you because these episodes say a lot about the essence of human beings, and in this specific case, the essence of woman. When she turned eighteen, as is the custom in Brazil, her parents organized a big party in which the young woman, who has reached the Rubicon of her life having come of age, receives gifts from her family and friends. The girl's name was Fabiola; she was gorgeous, blonde, with blue eyes and she must have been excited about the gifts she was about to get. It was the first big party of her life. The truth is that by her side I felt a little humiliated because I hadn't got a penny and had to ask her for money even to buy cigarettes. It was very tough.

– *Did she invite you to the family party?*

– No, she did much more. Without my knowing anything about it, she asked her friends and relatives to give her money instead of gifts. And when she had collected it all, she came to me and said, 'Paulo, your dream is the theatre. Well, you're going to have it. I've asked for money instead of gifts, and here you have it. Now you can try to realize your great hope.'

– *So you could start working in the theatre.*

– It didn't seem real to me. A new path opened before me. At first, she even helped me with my work. The years went by, I had found my feet and doors were opening for me. In the meantime, we stopped seeing each other. But one day, when I was working for TV Globo, which was the most important station in Brazil, writing texts and programme scripts, she showed up there.

– *She wanted to get back together?*

– No. It was much worse. She came to ask me a favour and I didn't do it. And at that moment God made me touch the bottom of my lack of generosity. I'll tell you. She came to me very happily and said, 'Paulo, you're not working in the theatre, but you're writing television scripts, how wonderful,' and added, 'I want to ask you a

favour. I know your director has a theatre and I'd like you to introduce me to him, since I'd like to become an actress.' This time my
past history was repeating itself – when I wanted to work in the
theatre and she helped me achieve it with an incredible generosity, giving up her presents.

– *And you had forgotten what she'd done for you?*

– It's not that I'd forgotten, but the truth is I was a coward, because
I didn't dare ask that favour of my director. And I said, 'Fabiola, I
can't help you.' And she went away sadly. I was very insensitive at
that time and only thought of myself, but a year later I realized
what I'd done and was terribly ashamed and in the depths of my
heart I hoped God would give me another opportunity to clear
my guilty conscience.

– *And did He?*

– Yes, Juan, because God first makes you see the worst of yourself
and then gives you a chance for redemption. In the end, Fabiola
changed her mind about going into the theatre and embarked on
a career as a sculptor, and triumphed, since she has a wonderful
talent. One day, by which time I was an established and famous
writer in Brazil, I ran into her in a bar. She said, 'How wonderful,
Paulo, that you're having such success with your books!' I felt

terribly ashamed after what had happened and I said, looking her in the eye, 'But how can you still be nice to me, when I was such a bastard to you?' But she just pretended not to hear. I didn't have to ask her to forgive me. It's what we were discussing the other day when we said the greatest largesse of spirit is when you don't need to forgive someone because you haven't felt offended, since forgiving is always in some way to feel yourself superior, humiliate the one you're forgiving.

– *She, rather than forgiving you, had generously forgotten everything so you wouldn't feel humiliated.*

– Without doubt. But she gave me a new opportunity. She said, 'Don't worry about the past, perhaps it was better I didn't go into acting. I'm happy now doing sculpture, and I want to ask you another favour.' I felt illuminated and said, 'Ask me anything, this time I won't let you down.' She told me her dream was to have a sculpture in one of the public squares in Río de Janeiro. I answered, 'Look, Fabiola, I don't care how much it costs, you shall have that statue, I am going to commission it and I'll find out about permission to erect it in a square and pay for it.'

– *And did you manage it?*

– Of course. It's in Our Lady of Peace plaza. If you want you can go see it there. The sculpture depicts two children, who are the two of us. She wanted it to have a plaque saying it was my donation. But I absolutely refused and told her, 'No, I'm not donating anything to you. You are the one giving me a possibility to make up for an old sin.' It is a very important story in understanding my life, that's why I wanted to tell you.

– *That woman gave you the chance to realize your best self as well as showing you your most negative side.*

– The fact is that all the women who've passed through my life have arrived at my door at a critical moment. They take me by the hand, put up with me, and make me change direction.

– *Your current wife, Cristina, too?*

– Absolutely. We've been together for eighteen years. She encouraged me to write. One day she said to me, 'You want to be a writer? Come on, we're going to travel.' I went through many important experiences and met many influential people thanks to her, and she's been wonderful company all the time. Later, when success arrived, she helped me to maintain my simplicity, to avoid arrogance. She has always accompanied me on my path, never fought against what I was searching for; she's respected me, supported me, injected me with enthusiasm each time I lost it, helped me get up when I fell.

Of course, we have our disagreements, like everyone. I now spend almost two hundred days of the year away from her, but I always feel her close and she lovingly cares for the foundation and fulfils herself in her painting which she truly loves.

— How did you meet?

— At a terrible moment. Because it was when I was practically possessed, I was involved in satanic sects. The first time she came to my house, I had a book about Satanism on the table. I asked her, 'What are you going to do today?' She told me she was going to sing in the square with the Evangelicals, because she was a member of that church then. I went to see her sing and was completely seduced. And since then she has accompanied me in my life. She knows I love women, but she doesn't hassle me about it, she stays faithful to her values and we are both together for love.

— And your previous partners?

— They were all better to me than I was to them. I've told you about Fabiola. My first wife was called Vera, she was Yugoslavian, quite a bit older than me. She was thirty-three when I was twenty-one. She taught me all the most important things about relationships, from sex to the capacity for dialogue. My second wife is the one I call my wife who shall be nameless, because she was the one kidnapped with me by the paramilitaries and with whom I was so cowardly, as I told you. The third, Cecilia, who I actually married, was someone very important to me. She was very young, she was nineteen and I was twenty-nine. She worked with me at the music company Polygram. Despite considering myself very normal back then, I treated her very badly and she suffered traumatic experiences. I was like that. However, I would never have amounted to anything without these women in my life, they were all much more mature than I was. Even today, as well as Cristina, my wife, who keeps me balanced, all my professional relationships are with women, from my literary agents to my editors. Women are always present in every moment of my life.

— It must be because you know how to connect with them. Not all men awaken this love in women. But what is the female aspect of your personality like?

— To tell you the truth, from the point of view of my interior feminine side, I had rather turned my back on that. Being the warrior I am, I like to join all battles, and I had fed my masculine side much more. Because of this I didn't know compassion or passion for life until I started to discover that I also have a woman within me, which is an extremely important dimension, without which we men will never be complete.

– *When did you start to become conscious of your need for your feminine side?*

– As I told you, I've struggled all my life against the obstacles I've found in my path. I took important decisions, like giving up drugs. But life got in the way. Sometimes I got irritated and said to myself, 'You don't know anything about life, you don't have control over anything.' And I tried to relax, let myself go. And in those moments when I did manage to let myself go, I'd feel better; it was as if I let life lead me, but soon problems would come up and I would notice I had to take control again, take decisions, that it wasn't enough to let myself drift along the river of life.

– *Until*

– Until after having made the pilgrimage to Santiago, which was the most intense experience of my life, I decided to do what in the RAM tradition – a very old spiritual tradition, over five hundred years old, born in the heart of the Catholic Church and to which I belong, along with four other disciples – is known as the 'feminine way'. Others call it the 'Road to Rome'. Its mission is to reveal the feminine side of our personality to us. From that experience came my book *Brida*, which is the story of a woman I met on that pilgrimage and whose experience was very close to my own. In some way, Brida is that woman I was looking for inside myself.

– *What exactly does this pilgrimage, the feminine way, consist of?*

– Many people might think it's silly, but for me those were seventy unforgettable, fundamental days. You set your own agenda, with no master telling you where you have to go. The main thing is to remember your dreams. Are not dreams ancestrally linked to the feminine soul? And during the day you have to realize your dream to the letter.

– *You had to interpret your dreams?*

– No, it wasn't about interpreting them, but about doing what you'd dreamt. If, for example, you'd dreamt about a bus station, you had to go to the nearest bus station and see what happened to you there. The same thing if you dreamt of a garage. One night I dreamt about football. Brazil and Denmark were playing. I dreamt that Denmark was going to win 3–2. When it was 2–2, I said 'There has to be another goal.' And there was, and the match finished 3–2, as I'd dreamt, except the reverse, because Brazil won.

– *What if you didn't dream?*

– I always dreamt something, because the same thing happens if you undergo psychoanalysis, it's not that you dream more, it's that you remember your dreams better. When I once told my master I hadn't dreamt at all, he said, 'Of course, you dreamt, you always dream something.' I answered him, 'Well, I dreamt of a garage.' And he told me, 'What do you want to dream of, the Virgin Mary? Go find a garage and see what happens.'

– Didn't you ever have the feeling you were making a mistake?

– Once I made a real mistake, and it almost cost me my life. I had dreamt of a name – Gez – which is the name of a mountain, and also of a chapel in a nearby town. But I believed the name referred to the mountain and I thought I had to go there. But it was a very difficult mountain to climb and I very nearly didn't make it back from there alive. The truth is I'd made a mistake, because it had to do with the chapel and not the mountain.

– Why is it called the feminine way?

– Because on this pilgrimage, – as opposed to the pilgrimage to Santiago, where according to the RAM tradition you especially develop your strength of will, based on discipline and personal effort – on the feminine way you especially develop compassion, meditation, approaching the roots of life, the earth. The pilgrimage to Santiago is more active, more of a battle. That's why I tend to say it's more 'Jesuitical', because the Jesuits were founded by Saint Ignacius de Loyola, who was a soldier. While the feminine way is more contemplative, that is, more 'Trappist', because those are the monks who devote themselves to meditation and discovering their inner abysses. It is a more feminine religiosity than the Jesuits', because Trappists work with their hands and cultivate gardens while undertaking lengthy meditations at the same time. Jesuits are more active and more involved in the battles of this earth.

– *In reality, the first goddess of history was feminine, the goddess Gaia, who was the goddess of the fertility of earth. Until, little by little, men, who were the warriors, made a masculine God. It was then that women began to be relegated to a secondary level and God became more like a severe lord, righteous, quick to punish, greedy for sacrifices.*

– That's why I don't like the way religions have robbed God of its feminine face, of compassion, love of life, of people and things. In fact, creation is a feminine process: slow and mysterious, not connected to our masculine logic, but to the essence of femininity, which is the protection of life and love, not of the wars that kill the fruit of her womb.

– *What do you mean by the 'feminine awakening'?*

– It's not at all a sexual expression, but rather one of freethinking, outside conventional logic. As you know, many writers use woman as a symbolic figure to explain the fusion between intuition and logic. Something that has a lot to do with dreams. Pontius Pilate's wife, according to the Gospels, had a dream that was not respected by her husband's rational logic, and he erred in not listening to her. And in *Julius Caesar*, Shakespeare had the wife of the would-be emperor alert him to the danger of going to the Senate on the ides of March. Julius Caesar, logically, thought a woman could understand very little of the political moment they were living through. He also erred.

– *And was it easy, the reunion with your feminine side?*

– No, it was slow and difficult, because gradually we have to rid ourselves of this culture that official knowledge has created in us, which is always masculine and which deprecates feminine values, as if no other philosophy than Descartes' has ever existed. The mystics have also existed, not seeing things exclusively through the eyes of Cartesian logic, of two plus two is four. Using only logic we lose contact with mystery, with the desire for the imaginary. That's why I love the Oriental philosophy of paradox, which is not that of the straight line, but of the circle, where something can be and not be at the same time, because life is not robotic with prefabricated answers. It's unpredictable and can change at any second.

– *With regard to the two plus two being four of classical materialism, the Spanish philosopher Fernando Savater, in a book of conversations like this one,* told me, 'sentimental reactions cannot be measured, while intelligence always operates with fixed quantities which can be calculated. Two plus two equals four in mathematics, while two sorrows plus two sorrows are not four sorrows, but could be what makes you throw yourself out the window.'

– That's magnificent.

– *What happens is our knowledge, especially in the West – less, for example in African cultures – is fundamentally masculine.*

– I am very fond of the tradition of the dove and the snake. Sometimes we need physical symbols to understand ourselves better. The classic image, which I like so much, is that of the Immaculate Virgin with a snake at her feet. The tradition of the Spirit, which departs from the principle that, what is important is not accumulation but knowing how to read the language of the collective unconscious, what we call the *anima mundi*. That would be the language of the dove. And then, on the other hand, the classical tradition of the snake, of the accumulation of wisdom. We cannot remain with one or the other exclusively, but must harmonize the two – logic and intuition.

– *Leonardo Boff, in his book* The Eagle and the Hen, *speaks of the African fable which alludes to what you're saying, because the eagle is part of the mystery of the heights we all have within, although we forget it, while the hen who flies close to the ground is the concrete, Cartesian logic, where there is little space for dreams and the supernatural and unexpected, but where there is also a reality that we have to count on.*

– Boff's book is lovely. And in the Gospels there are many examples of this, as when Jesus says he has come not to destroy law but to fulfil it in spirit. Because a time comes when respect and obedience to law keeps you from living, but you can't just live with anarchy either.

Another example from the Gospels that I like very much is when Jesus tells his disciples that when they go among men they should be 'wise as serpents and harmless as doves'. That's why we have to be alert and keep our feet on the ground, being concrete and objective, but at the same time knowing how to watch the run of things, enjoy contemplating them, trying to discover that secret language that speaks more to our unconscious feminine side, than to our reason.

– *You tend to speak of a feminine system of thought. What does it refer to?*

– I believe it is the opposite of what is usually called the Cartesian system of thought. To think in the feminine is to think in a different way from classic masculine logic, which has dominated thought for so long, especially Western thought.

– *What happens is that women, despite the battles fought to win their autonomy, are still ceded very little space in what you call the Academy, that is, by official wisdom. In Spain, for example, only one woman has ever been a rector of a university.*

– And she probably had superior masculine criteria than the men.

– *The great female politicians of history, from Golda Meir to Margaret Thatcher, have been very masculine women.*

– That is the big problem. That's why what I call the feminine system of thought is something else. Woman is sacred, she is feminine energy, she is what keeps us from building a wall between the sacred and the profane, she is the logic of mystery, of the incomprehensible, of miracles. I've already told you that on the feminine way, if you dream of a garage you have to go to one the next day, to see what happens to you. It is something lacking in logic, that's why it's closer to the imponderable, to the new, to what has to do with the deepest part of your being. That is the feminine to me.

– *We've agreed this century will certainly be more feminine, more womb-like, than the one that has just ended, more liquid and less solid. How do you see women's function in the near future?*

– The very same as men's. Because what I'm talking about is not women but the feminine. Look what happened with the most shattering feminist movements: they tried to conquer part of power, only then to wield it in a masculine way. That's not feminine. Women have to know how to balance their masculine and feminine energy, just as men also have to harmonize their two energies, the masculine and the feminine.

– *I wanted to ask you a question that we men talk very little about. We tend to say that we males have to discover the woman within because we're not only masculine. And, in fact, men are discovering their feminine sides which machismo had negated. But nevertheless, we don't accept that women have to discover their masculine sides, which they also have, we just want them to be feminine. It strikes me as very egotistical. Because we think we'll be more complete if we discover our feminine side, while we deny women the right to experience their masculine side, which they have. Does it seem fair to you?*

– Yes, Juan, I think I agree with you, but that's a problem that's neither mine nor yours, it's theirs. We have to stop being paternalistic with women. You're right, if we're discovering our femininity, it's only fair they should develop their masculinity, even though we might like them to be exclusively feminine. But they are the ones to wage that battle. They have to take up the sword and fight, we can't take their places. If they know how to fight, they'll discover what masculine energy is about.

— *We take it as given that women should just be feminine, and since we've conceived a society in which power requires masculine aptitudes, if we accept that women are fundamentally feminine, that they belong to the world of mystery, passivity, maximum artistic creativity, we automatically exclude them from positions of power.*

— You're right, but I still think it's not something we men can resolve. Women are the ones who have to realize it and fight to achieve it. Just as they had the first feminist revolution to get rid of discrimination, and, at least theoretically, to gain equal access to powerful positions, now they should unleash the second battle. When they achieve power, they should avoid wielding it as if it were exclusively male, because then they won't have achieved anything except replacing a man with a woman and nothing will change.

When a woman reaches a position of power, she should do everything possible to exercise it without forgetting her feminine characteristics, since all society's structures are fundamentally masculine and they have to break this mould, infiltrating it with feminine wisdom to construct a society in which positive elements can live side-by-side, masculine as much as feminine.

CHAPTER VI

Magic

❖

*'Black magic is diabolical because it makes
you believe you're all-powerful.'*

*'I consider myself a magus because I'm a person
who tries to develop his talents and power.
In that sense, everyone can be a magus.'*

❖

Before gaining fame as a writer, Paulo Coelho was known the world over as a magus, attributed with special powers. Today he prefers to be known as the author of books whose translation rights are fought over worldwide. He wanted to reveal in these conversations his painful past experiences, not just with drugs but with all kinds of magic, including the blackest, to which, he affirms, satanic rituals paled in comparison. He gave it up when he came to realize that those practices were leading him to the brink. He'd penetrated the very abysses of Evil. Coelho still believes in the magical dimension of life, considering each of us capable of developing the potential lying buried within us and that anyone who wants to can read the hidden, secret language of things in their essence.

— Do you still believe in the magical element of life?

— Totally.

— And what differences do you see between magic and the magical?

— Magic is a tool; the magical is the product of that tool. Magic is a space, it's like a hammer, a shovel, an instrument. How you use it is magical.

— Do you still feel yourself to be a magus? Many say that, in his day, Paulo Coelho was a magus.

– In his day, no. I am a magus, as all human beings are. Of course, I follow a Catholic spiritual tradition, but I firmly believe we all possess gifts we don't develop, because official wisdom, that empty space, refuses them, labels them superstitions or whatever. I'm a person who tries to develop my gifts and power, and that is what it means to be a magus, which doesn't make me any better or worse than the next person.

– *Well, let's explain a little further what you understand by magic before getting into your negative experiences in the past.*

– Look, what we're doing at this moment is, in some way, an act of magic, because it's a ritual which depends entirely on me and on whether I feel like telling you everything and trusting you or not. And to me, at this moment, you are not yourself but all my readers, you're all their curiosity. What you are going to do is interrogate me, which is your ability. It is the same as you did in your book on Saramago, *Possible Love*. When I read that book, I saw there were questions I would have liked to ask as a reader, to get to know that great Portuguese writer better. This kind of thing seems sacred to me, because it touches the intimate part of our being.

– *But you've also had experience with negative magic, black magic. How do you remember it?*

(At no time, during the length of our hours of conversation, was Coelho more tense and worried than when we touched on the theme of magic. It was midnight and he wanted to take a break before broaching the subject, because for him this time between day and night is a sacred and ritual hour. He was aware he was about to reveal key, painful moments of his life, and found it hard to begin. He asked, as well, since he was going to talk of magic, to be permitted to light some candles and turn off the electric light. And he did so.)

— So, we're going to talk about your experience with magic, a little-known world and perhaps your readers would be interested to know you spent time in that milieu.

— I'll try to explain it chronologically, to give an organized account, attempting to see myself while I speak. I've already told you about my negative experiences with drugs. I was educated by Jesuits, an education which gives one a certain concept of God. For me — I don't know about others — it was a rather negative experience overall, for it was in that Jesuit school that I lost my childhood faith. Because trying to impose a faith is the best way to make you rebel and go over to the other side. I've heard Fidel Castro also studied with Jesuits. For me, rebelling against that imposed religious education meant going over to Marxism. From there I began to read Marx and Engels.

– This was also the time of the Brazilian dictatorship.

– That's precisely why I began to read everything prohibited then. And one of the things I read was Marxist literature; it was considered demonic. I started reading everything. I felt like an atheist. But that experience of atheism lasted only for a short time because I had a writer's curiosity in my soul and began to ask myself the classic questions: Who am I? What am I doing here? Will I cease to be? Where did I come from? I don't know how old I was. It was around 1969, when the hippy movement started to take hold in Brazil along with all the mysticism that went along with it.

– And you were keen on that movement.

– I wondered: but what's this? At the beginning it seemed like a way of escaping reality, because at the time I was full of Marxist ideas and thought I was fighting for the people, for liberty, for the dictatorship of the proletariat, and all that, although in reality I felt riddled with contradictions, because I was fighting for a dictatorship of the proletariat; I went to demonstrations but at the same time I loved the Beatles. There was something in me beyond pure Marxism that made me say: Sergeant Pepper's! And I also loved the theatre.

– Deep down your search was more spiritual than political.

– The truth is I was attracted to the world of spiritualism and was looking for experiences that went further, since my traditional education of imposed religion hadn't convinced me. And so I went towards the furthest: I really got into Indian Cosmogony. I began reciting all the mantras to hand, practising yoga, meditating and everything related to oriental spirituality.

– *Were you single?*

– No, I was married to my first wife, and she had money and so I didn't have to worry about anything, except reading. I read the most diverse things, from *The Awakening of the Magus*, by Louis Pauwels and Jacques Bergier, to the literature of historic materialism. I was living in a hippy community at the time and a very strange thought occurred to me all of a sudden. I thought: if I'd been alive in 1928 and had been driving a car and at that moment Hitler went by and I'd run over and killed him by accident, would I really have changed millions of lives without knowing it? And the concrete reality is: they would have put me in jail for killing a man. He didn't know he was going to be Hitler, nor would I have known I'd killed a potential murderer of millions of people, but in reality I would have changed an entire structure, a whole society, an epoch, a world. That was when I started thinking about those things. I thought: that's crazy, I can't believe it, there really are more things that can happen on Earth than we could ever know about! With that and the influence of Indian mythology I began to live through different experiences, as do all people who initiate a spiritual quest.

— And that was when you began to seek out masters to initiate you on that quest, when you yourself didn't even know what it was yet.

— That's right. We put all our hopes and confidence in a figure who ended up deceiving us, but at that initial moment he was important, even indispensable to us, for he led us by the hand through the labyrinths and mysteries of life. I then began to fall into the hands of several masters, from many different sects, many different philosophies, until the day when my extremist personality led me to search out the most intense, what was the far-left of the far-left of spiritual quest.

— You wanted to distinguish yourself from your friends by looking for different things.

— Yes, for that and for another reason that strikes me as very silly now: I wanted to seduce women, I wanted to impress them with my knowledge of the strangest things. I wondered, which secret society is considered the black sheep, the most intense? I was told about a sect whose name I do not wish to pronounce. I'll call it the aperture of the Apocalypse. I had a great mentor.

— And you surrendered yourself to him.

— I started reading everything I could find about him. I had already been through a lot of other experiences and it was when I was trying to write and was founding an alternative press. It was when I had my magazine, which I told you about. I needed to find out as much as I could as quickly as possible about that character and I went to interview someone for the magazine, thinking he could help me. To my surprise, that man, who must have known a lot about the subject, had hardly any books. I was surprised, because I was used to knowledgeable people having lots of books.

(At this moment in the conversation his wife, Cristina, took out her camera to take a photo of us. Coelho said to her, 'Cristina, don't take pictures. We're talking about magic and magi say the image has fantastic powers. As a matter of fact, Castaneda never allowed himself to be photographed. He died leaving no photos. I'm not Castaneda, but still …' Cristina didn't pay any attention to him and pressed the button. It was night-time and the flash didn't work. 'There, you see,' he commented, 'we're talking about magic and your photo didn't come out. Please, Cristina, don't distract me, I'm telling very intimate details of my life.')

— Let's get back to this person you went to interview about that black magic sect for your magazine.

– I realized my conversation with him was very fruitful and the three or four books he did have looked very interesting. I asked him who they were by and he said Aleister Crowley. I imagine you've heard of him, because he has influenced a great many people. I'd gone to see this man with my wife, the wife I won't name, and we were fascinated.

– *What was that secret sect like?*

– It's a society which was formed at the beginning of the nineteenth century and its aim is 'the total quest united with total anarchy', something that for a young man of twenty-three, as I was, sounded like a perfect ideal. I once wrote about this experience, from my getting to know Raúl to just before prison, and Cristina wouldn't let me publish it. She read it because she didn't know the story. She read it with great interest and when she was almost at the end she looked at me like an image of Our Lady of the Apparition and said to me, 'Don't publish this book, this book is about evil, your experience with evil.' I said, 'But Cristina, it's just a tragic experience.' And she insisted, 'It's fascinating, but don't publish it because it could be very badly interpreted.' And I erased the book from my computer. I spent a night in terror and the next day – I had already printed almost the whole book – we went out to dinner with the publisher, who I told, ' Have a look at this, because you're the last person who's going to read it.'

He looked at me as if I were crazy. I told him I was going to destroy it. And I did. I only kept one chapter telling the story of my meeting Raúl. The rest I threw away.

— *What was it called?*

— *The Alternative Society*. Anyway, I have to tell you a bit about Crowley, so you'll understand things better, a very odd character in the history of magic. The only thing I'm not going to give you is the name of the secret society I joined. I'll tell you what happened to me in it. If you see his face on the Internet, you'll see it is the face of evil. Crowley was an evil man, with a very strong personality who showed up in a decadent moment in classical magic, where there were secret societies, freemasonry and some English occult groups. This man arrived and said, 'no more secrets', and started publishing all the books that up until then had been kept secret and he formed his own society. With this society he created social, political and ideological systems, which had a key book — like all systems of the kind, like *Das Kapital* or the Gospels — called *The Book of the Law*, and which he claimed was dictated to him by an angel in Cairo.

— *What does it propose?*

— It contains a declaration of principles, which is very lucid, like all of Crowley's work. He began developing a system of power relations that can be summed up as follows: there are the weak and the strong, and the law of the jungle. The weak are slaves, and the strong are powerful and free. All this is expressed in extremely solid, magical and mystical writing. Both fascinating and irresponsible, I began practising those teachings and they soon gave good results.

(On Aleister Crowley's Web page it says: 'Enigmatic and constantly criticized, not only during his own lifetime, characterized by prevailing Victorian morality, when he came to be known as "the wickedest man in the world", but even today his name still evokes, among those who believe they know the Man and his System, an aura of malignity and perversion, labelling him unjustly as a Black Magus or, even more absurdly, if possible, a Satanist. What is often left out or played down in his biographies, is that Aleister Crowley was a man committed to a kind of spiritual search, who in reality was a Magus in the widest sense of the word.')

— *At the time you blindly believed in that sect.*

— To be completely honest, I believed and I didn't believe, I believed without believing, although I was seduced. That was when I first crossed paths with Raúl Seixas. It's as if everything happened at once. So I took Raúl to the secret society, which was totally open, free of rules, you could be a monster or a marvellous person. Everyone fitted in there. I remember there was total sexual freedom, freedom of thought, everything, including oppression. It was about taking the experience of power to its maximum limits.

— And didn't it frighten you?

— The truth is I looked at it all without completely believing in it, or I only saw its positive side then. I was very impressionable and I sensed big changes in my life and in the lives of other members of that sect. And later I started to realize what separates white magic from black magic is sometimes something very subtle. But it's as concrete as this: in black magic, you try to interfere in the destiny of others.

That is the border, the limit and the abyss. You might go into a church, light a candle to Our Lady and say, 'I want to marry so-and-so.' In that case, what you're doing is black magic, even though you're in a Catholic church. Or you can go to a crossroads and leave food for demons and ask them for them to heal you, because you don't feel well. And that's white magic, because you're not trying to influence anyone else's destiny. The issue is interfering, or not, in the lives of others. But it would be better if you ask me questions, because this is all very delicate.

– Don't worry. Just tell me as it comes to you.

– All that had great symbolic value to me, they were like symbols in motion. Then, Raúl and I decided we had to put our music to the secret society's use, and we did. Behind the lyrics were the sect's declarations of principles although very subliminally. They were like a series of precise and perfect mantras; because evil, Juan, is very precise.

– How did you begin to see it as the domination of evil?

– At that time I didn't yet see it as a bad experience, I saw it as revolutionary, because Crowley claimed to be the aperture of the Apocalypse, 'I am life, I am the awaited life, I have come to change all of society.' I saw it as something good and positive. And I went through a whole series of rituals, although I rejected some, because I didn't want to give up certain of my childhood devotions like my guardian angel or devotion to Saint Joseph.

– Was the sect very anti-religious?

– Yes, totally anti-religious. At the time, I was very anti-Catholic myself, as I've told you, I'd abandoned the faith of my parents, but deep down I hadn't given up certain aspects of my old faith.

— When did you begin to realize that the sect incarnated evil in some way?

— One day, before I was imprisoned — I have the phone numbers of witnesses you can ask about this — I was in my house when all of a sudden everything started to go black. I had something specific to do that day, I can't remember what. The woman I won't name wasn't home, and I said to myself, 'it must be residual effects of some strange drugs from the past', but I'd given up drugs, this was in 1974. I was doing a bit of cocaine then, but I wasn't taking psychotropic drugs anymore.

— And what exactly happened to you?

— It was very early and I started, as I said, to see everything black and to feel I was going to die. It was a very concrete, physical, visible blackness. It wasn't my imagination, it was tangible. My first impression was that I was dying.

— What was the blackness like? Could you see anything?

— Yes, I could see, because it didn't take up all the space, just part of it. It was as if this candle suddenly started smoking and the smoke invaded the house, a black, black smoke that got thicker and at times you could barely see a thing, but which most of all caused you to panic.

— Were there any other phenomena? Was it just smoke?

— No, perhaps worst of all was a series of noises that I don't know how to describe to you, at the same time as that black smoke was forming.

— Were you with someone or alone?

— I was completely alone. The flat was my property, I thought I was rich, happy. But the darkness that covered half the space from the floor to the ceiling terrorized me and I ended up completely out of control. I was panicking; I recognized it as the presence of Evil. Initially, I established a relation between that and a woman I was seeing at the time. I had undergone some episodes of suggestion with her, but also some very positive things for me, although not for the others.

— And how did you react faced with that strange phenomenon?

— I can't remember now if I called someone or if a woman from the group called me, I think she had called me and said the same thing was happening to her. And so I understood it was something real, not a hallucination. Also, she was the one who knew the most about the sect. We couldn't get in touch with the guru because he didn't have a telephone; it was very hard to get one in Río in 1973.

I was in a state and very startled. I tried to react and said to myself: I have to forget about it, fill my head with something to get rid of the fear. But the darkness was still there, it didn't disappear. Then, to distract myself, I decided to count the records I had in the house, there were lots, and I'd never counted them. And when I finished counting the records I started counting the books, but the blackness remained unchanged.

— And when you finished counting everything in your house, what did you do?

— Since I was still gripped by fear, I thought the only solution was to go to a church, but a kind of force kept me from leaving the house and I had very strong premonitions of imminent death. At that moment, the woman I was with then, who belonged to the same sect, arrived. She had just had the same experience of the blackness. And bit by bit we found out that we were all experiencing the same thing, including Raúl. I felt the presence of Evil as something visible and tangible. It was as if Evil had said to me, 'You invoked me, here I am.'

— How long were you in that sect?

— About two years. I remembered that at other times, when my wife and I were really into drugs, what a relief it was to drink milk or splash water on our faces. But at that moment, neither she nor I could get up the courage to go into the bathroom, we didn't dare cross that horrible darkness. In the end we talked ourselves into it; we splashed a little water on our faces and felt a bit better. Then we thought of taking a shower. We did, but when we came out it was still the same, that menacing, mysterious blackness was still there. And, at that moment, all my childish religious beliefs came back to my mind. The issue right then was not so much whether I was going to die, but having proof of the existence, the visible reality, of that mysterious energy.

– *In any of the rituals of that secret society, had you invoked the Evil One?*

– Always, but understanding Evil as the great rebellion not as the Evil One.

– *Was it a satanic sect?*

– Compared to what went on there, satanic rituals, which I was quite familiar with, were nothing. This was much more dangerous.

– *More dangerous than the Church of Satan?*

– Much more, because it was a more philosophical sect, more structured, more dangerous in its roots. All conventional magic rites were performed there, but that was the kingdom of pure power. Sometimes we invoked Evil with very concrete results, but never anything as visible as that blackness that invaded my house.

— What did you commit yourselves to through those rites and invocations?

— To nothing. We had all the power, the demon's great game is the same as cocaine, it makes you believe you have all the power; that's why I identify the energy of cocaine with this, because cocaine gives you the same feelings of power, of domination, of total security, but in appearance only. The truth is you're the slave.

— Let's get back to that experience. How did it end?

— In the end I picked up a Bible. It was a Saturday. I opened it at random and there was a passage in the Gospel in which Jesus asks someone if he believes, and he answers, 'Lord, I believe, help thou mine unbelief.' It was by reading this passage and making a promise like the one I made a short time later about drugs. I said to myself, 'I'm through with this sect forever.' And it all disappeared. Later, talking with my other friends in the secret society, I found we'd all had the same experience.

— How did you manage to escape from the association that had trapped you?

– I went to speak to one of the gurus of the sect and he told me it was a rite of initiation. I told him, 'I don't care, from this moment forward, count me out.' My master wasn't there and so I sent him a telegram. Indeed, it was a very difficult telegram to compose, because it was right in the middle of the dictatorship and everything was censored. In the annals of that secret society there are many references to me; I think they say the worst possible things, because they have my letters, my articles, thousands of my things.

– *They never persecuted you for having left?*

– Never. But I don't want to talk about that right now because it's past midnight. We'll continue later ... What they did do was put pressure on me by saying that I was a coward, that I was stupid, that I knew what I would be losing. But persecute me, no. I don't believe what I sometimes see on television about sects pursuing those who leave them, sometimes to the death. I don't believe it.

– *It seems there are sects that do.*

– In the real sects, it is a privilege to be there, but if you leave nothing happens. At least, I've never been pursued and that was one of the most dangerous, toughest sects in existence.

— But, despite that terrible experience with black magic, you still consider yourself a magus. Don't you think this could in some way obscure your image as a renowned writer?

— No, because I conceive of being a magus in a very different way, that is, as a force we all possess, at least potentially. Being a magus means developing a cognitive power not always accepted by official wisdom. A magus is a normal person, but one who is aware of other realities, other movements, other currents beneath the surface of things.

What's hidden behind appearances, that secret language things possess, is invisible, and just as real as love, but nevertheless we can't touch it.

— Do you consider that dimension of magic as a hidden power?

— On the contrary. The true magus is the one who, as Jesus Christ said, struggles to bring things out of hiding. His function is to reveal what the powerful try to keep hidden, unmask the societies that play with secrets to control a person's will by offering them a false power that is merely destructive.

In this society, Juan, there are many people who use secrets to dominate others. That's why the one who controls the most information has the most power. I saw a work, I think it was a play, about a revolution, and who should they choose to be Minister of

Culture but the censor, since he was the one who knew everything, for he controlled it all. The true magus does not allow himself to be subjugated by the cliques who claim to know everything, because they think they can hold all the world's knowledge.

– *One thing is certain, Paulo, and it's that many people fear magic.*

– And they do so wisely, because magic can be very dangerous. I would say it's like nuclear energy, it depends on the uses you put it to. You can make atomic bombs or generate light with it. So not all nuclear energy is good, nor are all types of magic. You need to know how to tell the difference.

– *A question remains unanswered. Do you believe in the personification of the demon?*

– I believe in the personification of the artificial demon.

– *What do you mean by that?*

– That there is a demon who is the left hand of God and another that is the product of the collective unconscious which personifies it. What, for example, is a word? It is the personification of a thought. So then, in the same way you personify love by saying the word 'love', you can personify the demon by invoking it. But, at the same time as you turn on the light you destroy it, because it has no more power than you yourself give it.

— But you saw the personification of the demon with your own eyes.

— But it was because I had granted it power before. But now it has no power over me, because I have denied it. And now, Juan, I'd like to talk about something else …

CHAPTER VII

Drugs

*'It's not true that drugs are horrible, as they say
in the campaigns. Drugs are bad because
they're fantastic.'*

*'Cocaine is the demon's drug,
because it makes you feel omnipotent.'*

Some of Coelho's friends have tried to cover up one of the most painful chapters of the writer's past: his involvement with drugs. Or they try to minimize it, as if drugs had been a fleeting and insignificant phase in his life. He does not agree. He does not wish to hide this dark part of his past, which took him to the brink of death, as he recounts with tremendous sincerity in these conversations. He was left so scarred by his past experience that he now considers himself a conservative on this issue and is against the decriminalization of drugs. But he also criticizes the anti-drugs policies that generate certain kinds of advertising campaigns because he believes it is a lie to tell young people that drugs are horrible. It is a lie, says Coelho, because it's not true. On the contrary, drugs are enormously dangerous and difficult to give up precisely because of their appeal. And young people need to know that something which produces such pleasant effects will end up converting them into worthless lumps of humanity, destroying their control over their own will.

— *What was it that led you to give up drugs once and for all?*

— You don't give up drugs from one day to the next. In my case I gave them up in stages. The toughest periods of my life, when I was totally involved in all kinds of drugs and hallucinogens, even the strongest and most dangerous, were during the 1970s. And I gradually gave them up for various different reasons.

— Why are you so opposed to the current campaign against drugs?

— Because they are committing absolute outrages, just as much with drugs as with tobacco. The worst thing you can do with these things is demonize them, as if they were horrible, disagreeable, meaningless. To my way of thinking this is just going to throw a whole generation into the arms of drugs.

— Why?

— Because all you have to do to attract young people to drugs is say they're bad for them. I believe very strongly in the power of rebellion, because without it we don't live. And youth is rebellious in principle and physiologically.

— Why did you get into drugs?

— Precisely to rebel, because they were forbidden and everything forbidden fascinated me. It was, for me and for the youth of '68 in general, a way of answering back to our parents' generation. We answered back in many ways and one of them was with drugs. I was always a person of extremes who never took half measures; I still am, thank God. That's why I like what it says in the Bible, 'I would thou wert cold or hot. ... because thou art lukewarm, ... I will spew thee out of my mouth.'

I've already told you I like to be a warrior of the light, wage battles, that's why I find it difficult to conceive of a universe in harmony. For me, the sun is a symbol of what I'm saying. The sun, which is life and light to us, is not at all harmonious, it is a huge atomic explosion, if we approach it we die.

— So, you got into drugs out of rebellion, because it was forbidden and presented a way of protesting against the confining society of the time. Why did you give them up?

— As I said, I gave them up for different reasons. The main one was fear. I had gone very far: cocaine, hallucinogens, LSD, peyote, mescaline, plus other pharmaceutical products. I began by giving up the strongest and then just took cocaine and marijuana. However, I now consider cocaine to be the demon's drug, it is satanic energy which gives you the false impression of omnipotence while it's destroying you, wresting away your decision-making ability.

— But at the time you didn't realize it?

— No, I consumed cocaine unceasingly and nothing happened. I took it with my friends. Curiously, it didn't have a big effect on me. I felt it as a fantastic thing; as if acquiring enormous power, I felt a great sensation of strength and well-being.

– But you suffered a terrible feeling of paranoia.

– Yes, it was when I got out of prison the third time. And when Raúl Seixas and I decided to go to New York. My paranoia was so great that I couldn't possibly live here in Río de Janeiro. If I went out I'd think someone was following me, if I talked on the phone I'd be sure someone was listening. I remember during the World Cup in 1974, I thought I could go outside because Brazil was playing Yugoslavia. I thought all the streets would be empty because everyone would be watching the match, particularly the soldiers, and that no one would follow me. I said to myself, 'Either I go out today or I'll never go out again in my life.' I was scared out of my wits.

– But you went out.

– Yes, and I remember the streets were deserted. I looked both ways and said to myself, 'If anyone follows me, I'll notice right away.' But a time came when my paranoia was so great that I couldn't live like that, I couldn't. So that's when I decided to travel to the States. That was when I left everyone, all my friends. I was very disloyal to them. Raúl understood completely; he thought if he had suffered the paranoia I did, he probably would have done the same thing. But in the end he found it catching and that was when we both decided to go to New York and we left Brazil.

— But you kept doing drugs there.

— Yes, cocaine was still the drug of the moment, although it still didn't give me any great highs. Instead, I continued to suffer from paranoia and delusions of omnipotence.

— And it was in New York where you experienced the full power of the drug.

— Yes, I remember it perfectly, because it was the day Nixon resigned as President of the United States, 8 August. I had a girl-friend there and we were staying in the Village and we both snorted coke. And it was the first time, after a year of taking it that I noticed the drug's full power. That's why I tell you the anti-drugs campaign is mistaken. Cocaine is bad because it produces unpredictable effects. That day, I experienced the drug with an enormous inten-sity. We watched Nixon's resignation and then we went out for a walk in Times Square and from there to a discotheque.

— And when did you realize what was going on?

— We had come back from the disco and it was nine o'clock in the morning, not having been able to sleep — curiously, there hadn't been any sex. I remember my girlfriend lying naked on the bed. At that moment I had an inspiration. I said to myself, 'If I keep taking cocaine like this, I'm going to destroy myself.' I remember I went to look out the window and the street was empty. It wasn't anything concrete, it was a very strong feeling that I'd started down the path to my death. Up until then I'd felt very calm, because although I'd seen many of my friends destroyed, drugs had never had much of an effect on me. But that day I realized that if I didn't stop, I'd end up like them ...

— *And you decided to stop.*

— Yes, at that moment, and in front of my naked girlfriend on the bed, I made a pledge, something I've rarely done in my life. I said to myself, 'From this day forward, never again in my life will I touch cocaine.' And look, Juan, when it comes to drugs, that is a very difficult thing to say, 'Never again in my life.'

— *And have you been faithful to your pledge?*

— So far. I still smoked marijuana then, but nothing else. But I stuck to the oath to give up cocaine forever. I haven't made that pledge with tobacco, and I still smoke even though I know it's not good for me. But no more drugs. That's why I'm telling you about that 8 August, the day Nixon resigned, it was a very important day for my future life.

— *But you eventually gave up marijuana too.*

– Yes, it was when I was with my wife, Cristina, in Amsterdam. I began to notice it always gave me the same feeling, which really wasn't much of anything. It wasn't worth carrying on, it was better to stop. And since then, 1982, Paulo Coelho has not touched a single illicit drug.

– *Why do you think today's youth still go for drugs in such a big way?*

– I think for the same reason we did, although there may also be others: because older people tell them it's so horrible. Then they smoke a spliff and realize it's not at all horrible, it even makes them better lovers.

– *So what should they be told?*

– That it's dangerous because of that, because drugs produce fantastic effects and don't let you see how they're destroying you little by little, annulling your willpower, converting you into an automaton and a slave, incapable of deciding for yourself in life anymore. That's why I've said they're diabolical, because it's a huge trap, a big lie. I remember my experiences with that woman they kidnapped and tortured with me. We spent twenty-four hours a day under the effects of all kinds of drugs. We were unhinged. We travelled to the United States with drugs in our luggage, risking prison. We didn't care, we were totally thoughtless.

I don't know how I would have ended up if I'd kept on that road. Probably like some of my poor friends ended up …

I told you that cocaine is the demon's drug, very dangerous. What happens is there's a lot of hypocrisy and irresponsibility in many of the people who speak to the young about drugs, because they're the ones who haven't tried them and so they're speaking out of ignorance, about something they know nothing about.

(Cristina interrupts the conversation to tell us about an advertisement against drugs showing a kind of lizard that went up a person's nose and ate their brain. And she contrasted it to a more serious advert she'd seen in England which gave advice to those involved in drugs so they'd do themselves as little damage as possible if they couldn't manage to quit.)

— That's a great idea. I have to talk to a friend of mine who's in advertising to tell him about it. What you can't do is deceive young people. And I think the advertising they're using today, instead of stopping drug use it encourages it.

— *What do you say on the subject when young people ask for your opinion in public?*

— I always say that I'm opposed, because I have experienced the danger myself. And I am so opposed that I feel quite conservative and do not agree with those who say it should be decriminalized, although it may seem contradictory, because I've said that drugs are attractive because they're forbidden. But, in spite of everything, after my own difficult experience, I'd rather they stayed illegal.

CHAPTER VIII

Conversion

❖

*'The bells of that concentration camp
were tolling for me.'*

❖

At thirty-four years of age, having given up most of his youthful adventures, Paulo Coelho set off on a trip with his wife, Cristina, in search of a new spiritual path. And on that journey, in the most unexpected place, at Dachau, the Nazi concentration camp, he underwent a very powerful spiritual experience, which set his life definitively back towards Catholicism. It must have been a very intense experience. Twenty years later, retelling it for this book in the small hours of the morning, Coelho couldn't hold back his emotions and we had to interrupt the recording when he burst into tears.

— *You were thirty-four years old when you finally decided to be a serious, focussed person.*

— Yes, too many things had happened and I'd done too many crazy things in my life. My wife, the one I won't name, the one who was tortured with me by the paramilitaries and with whom I was such a coward, as I told you, had left me. My third marriage, with Cecilia, had also finished. Then, in 1979, I married Cristina. Then I got fired from Polygram where I worked. But I didn't have financial problems, I owned five apartments and had seventeen thousand dollars in my bank account. I started to feel curiosity again about something that I had distanced myself from entirely in my out-of-control life.

— *And you set off travelling again.*

— Exactly. I was very dissatisfied with my life and I said to Cristina, 'Look, I'm thirty-four, soon I'm going to be old, so let's live, let's travel the world, let's look for the meaning of life, let's go back to the places I went when I was young.' So we set off on a great journey.

— Where did you go?

— We went to several countries, including Germany. Little Paula, my niece, Cristina's sister's daughter, had just been born. We also went to the communist countries. I still held to my socialist ideals and wanted to see that reality close up. We bought a car in Yugoslavia, at the Indian embassy. And from there we went back to Germany because Cristina's sister was living there. The car, which we weren't really allowed to buy, was a Mercedes that cost us a thousand dollars; it was perfect, beautiful, but with diplomatic plates. What we did was change the licence plates in Germany, and hey presto. It was a great trip. We got to Germany, Cristina's sister lived in Bonn, but we stayed in Munich, because I'd always been very interested in the Second World War.

— And it was in Germany that you went to visit a former concentration camp.

— Yes, since I'd never been in one of those camps, I was very interested to visit. We went to Dachau. As you've been there yourself, I don't need to tell you much. I remember that it was a Sunday and

I don't know why but I think we went to mass that day. Then we drove to Dachau and parked the car. There was no one around. It was a Sunday in February, zero degrees and a freezing wind cut into our faces. There was nobody in the museum, not even an attendant, we looked around and I began to feel very deeply moved.

– *It's true, the first time you go to one of those camps you feel your blood run cold. I remember a visit to a cell in Auschwitz, in Poland, and I'll never in my life forget that impression.*

– I had only seen these places in films, but the reality was so different, so deep and horrid. There was a room for relatives who had lost family members there and that particularly affected me, because if the camp represented the past, that was the present. Then we visited the house of the camp commandant and a small barracks. Everything was desolate. And when we came out on the left, the opposite: exuberant vegetation, a river and the old crematoria.

– *I didn't have the courage to enter a crematorium. I consider them evil, the degradation of humanity.*

– I exclaimed, 'How dreadful!' and my imagination started to work. I shut myself up in one of the gas chambers to see what I felt. There was a different light, pretty, a morning light, a complete contrast.

– *The contrasts in concentration camps that you mention are chilling. I can't forget in Auschwitz, there was a rusty pipe where water must have come out in the times of horror, and beside it was growing a tiny wild flower, perhaps embracing some drop of water that had trickled out.*

– When I came out of the shower block, it was exactly noon. My wife and I went outside and started towards the car, which we'd left parked near the guard's hut. If you recall, at the end of Dachau are three chapels, a Catholic one, a Jewish one and another, Protestant I guess. We went into the Catholic one, lit a candle and then went in the direction of the car, which was quite far away; we had to walk a long way and it was terribly cold.

The bells began to chime while we were walking, marking midday.

– *The same bells that once tolled to summon the prisoners to gather in the camp.*

– Exactly. And my imagination flew. As a writer I'm used to creating atmosphere, I imagined the barracks heaving with prisoners, all that degradation of humanity. I walked trying to decrease the terrifying impression and at a certain point I stopped and read on the guard's hut: 'Never again.' That calmed me for a moment, thinking it wouldn't happen again, because it was impossible man could repeat that barbarism.

— Unfortunately, it's not been the case.

— That's what I suddenly began to understand, that it wasn't true it wouldn't be repeated, because in reality it was happening again at that very moment. I myself had experienced in my own flesh the horror of one human being torturing another, submitting you to the most humiliating torments without being able to do a thing to defend yourself. I thought of the dirty wars, of people dying at that very moment in El Salvador. I remembered that the same horrors were happening to the Mothers of the Plaza del Mayo, in Argentina[5], I thought of soldiers throwing innocent people out of aeroplanes, and of all the horrors perpetrated in dictatorships' dungeons.

— And you realized that man was still just as mad and miserable.

— And suddenly I felt desperate, impotent and absolutely terrifyingly useless. I thought: these sons of bitches of human beings never learn anything; we're condemned to repeat the same

[5] Argentinian protest group founded by women whose children had disappeared under the military regime and who brought their frequent protests to the Plaza de Mayo in Buenos Aires. The early protests faced threats and intimidation from the military police; subsequent events were met with arrests and violence; the organization driving the plaza protests was infiltrated and several of their leaders disappeared, but they are still an active force in Argentinian politics.

horrors, because what happened in Germany in 1945 happens now on my own continent. But at the same time I thought it wasn't possible that mankind didn't learn the lessons of the past. I began, as if I were reading a book, to repeat something another writer had said, 'No man is an island.' I wondered where I'd read that. 'No man is an island.' What book had I read that in? ... But, bit by bit, the whole paragraph came to mind: 'Europe is the less ... any man's death diminishes me ...' I kept saying to myself, but who wrote it? I had the whole piece committed to memory, and the last line, 'never send to know for whom the bell tolls; it tolls for thee'. Then I realized, I was in the middle of a concentration camp with bells tolling and it was a very strong emotion, because I suddenly understood, as in a moment of illumination, that those bells were tolling for me.

(Here we had to interrupt the recording because Paulo Coelho broke down in tears. After a few seconds, as if wanting to play down his emotions, he said he was sorry and added, 'Perhaps I've had too much to drink.')

And that, Juan, was not just a symbolic act because in that very instant, when I discovered the bells were tolling for me and that I too had to do something with my life to stop the horror of a humanity that doesn't learn the lessons of its madness, I heard a voice and saw a person. I saw someone and they disappeared.

I didn't have time to speak to the person because they vanished so quickly but the image remained perfectly engraved on my memory.

— And what did you do?

— I went back to the car, told the story, cried. But as humanity and all men have the same tendencies, the next day I'd forgotten it. I didn't know for whom the bells tolled anymore, I thought it had just been one more experience in my life.

— But that wasn't the case?

— No. Two months went by and we kept travelling, then one day, in Amsterdam, we decided to stay there, in a hotel that doesn't exist any more, because it was an illegal hotel, but very cheap and fantastic. We were there when I said I was going to stop smoking marijuana and Cristina took her first and last tab of LSD. The hotel had a bar downstairs. I was having a coffee there with Cristina when, at a certain point, someone else came in for coffee and I said, 'I know that person, but I don't know where from.' Suddenly, I remembered that I'd seen them at the concentration camp. But I was frightened, for I thought they might be pursuing me because of what happened in 1974, when I was involved in black magic. But at the same time I was curious and thought if I didn't speak to him, he'd go and I wouldn't meet him again.

— And you went to speak to him?

— Yes, I stood up and said, 'I saw you a couple of months ago.' He looked at me, and answered in English, 'Are you crazy?' 'No, no, I'm not crazy, I saw you two months ago,' I told him. I was sort of upset, because the whole experience at the concentration camp suddenly came back to me. And at the same time I'd heard that sects sometimes pursue those who leave them, although I'd never believed it. He told me to sit down, and started asking a series of questions. While he was talking, I was getting more and more convinced that it had to do with the concentration camp, that this was the person I'd seen there like an apparition.

— And what did he tell you?

— He said, 'Look, maybe you did see me, but there's such a thing as astral projection, because you couldn't have seen me before. They're things that happen when you take hallucinogens.' And I kept coming up with excuses so he wouldn't leave, for I felt this was an important person in my life. He kept talking to me about astral projection but eventually said, 'I think you have a few problems you haven't resolved yet, and if you want I can help you. I work for a multinational company, my name's Jean, if you want I can give you a hand, but you have to tell me sincerely if you do or don't want my help.' I told him I'd have to think about it. 'I always have coffee here at this time of day, tomorrow you can give me your answer, but if you wait until the day after I'll assume you don't want my help,' he said. 'You've got twenty-four hours to think it over.'

I was really in a mess at the time, because I didn't know if he was a good or bad person. I talked to Cristina, I couldn't sleep all night. I felt totally confused.

— And in the end what did you decide?

— I decided to say 'yes'. And a new stretch of my life started there, with my return to the Catholic Church. That person belonged to the ancient Catholic RAM order (Rigour, Adoration, Mercy). He was the one who told me all about the tradition, of the symbolic anchor within a church. He had spent a lot of time in the Vatican. And after that I began to take an interest in that ancient Catholic tradition, and the tradition of the serpent, until one day he took me to Norway and gave me this ring, which I still wear, with the two-headed snake. And then I began to learn the symbolic language that isn't Christian esoterica, but the Christian system of symbols.

— Does the Church accept it?

— It is a very ancient tradition.

(At that precise moment, Cristina found a small white feather under the table where we were talking, the dining room table. She picked it up and handed it to her husband. 'What's this?' 'A white bird's feather.' Visibly moved, Coelho thanked his wife and explained that, for him, the sudden appearance of that feather in an unexpected place was a sign of the impending birth of a new book. And we were then reaching the end of our conversations.)

— Joining the order of RAM reconciled you with Catholicism. But this is a very little-known order. Has it many members?

— People who believe and act within it speak very little of our experiences. It is an order founded over five centuries ago, within the Catholic Church. Symbolic language is passed down through an oral tradition. But it's not at all secret. RAM is more of a practice of the sacred than a theory of it. That's why we're such a small group. In fact, it still has only four disciples.

CHAPTER IX

The Writer

—❧—

'My process of literary creation resembles that of
a pregnant woman who has to give birth to
a new creature.'

'For inspiration, I have to make love with life.'

—❧—

If Paulo Coelho was known for many years primarily as a well-respected magus, credited with special powers, today his standing comes primarily from being a writer. And it is precisely this literary standing that many critics go out of their way to deny him, cataloguing his books as self-help manuals or esoterica. Coelho defends his simplicity as a tool to reach all audiences. He considers himself a storyteller and believes his books should be placed on the Philosophy or Literature shelves in bookshops. To those who allege that his books contain grammatical errors, he answers that there were also critics who found them in Don Quixote. What no one denies is that he is one of the ten best-selling authors in the world, with more than twenty-two million copies sold by September 1998, despite the fact that his literary production is quite recent, with barely twelve books published. In just a few years Coelho has sold more books than Jorge Amado did throughout his whole long life. He speaks of his creative process as a writer in these conversations, affirming that in order to write he needs to make love with life.

— *Why do you feel the need to write?*

— Because I believe the only way to share our personal love is through work, and writing is my work, just as a cabby's is driving.

— *Do you feel writing imposed itself on you or did you choose it?*

— I chose it and I've dreamt of it all my life. I've always pursued it, stumbling, often making mistakes, but I triumphed through the force of my will, and this has always been my motto.

— *You've said you need to connect with the centre of energy in order to write. What do you mean?*

— I like to use terms from alchemy, which is the soul of the world, or those of Jung's collective unconscious. You connect with a space where everything is.

— *Borges often spoke of that.*

— Borges called it the Aleph, the point where all things are. Aleph is a Hebrew word, from the Kabbalah, the first letter of the alphabet. It is the point that embraces all things at once. In Borges' story called 'The Aleph', a man is walking, he trips and falls, and completely by accident enters this point where he sees everything at the same time: all the people, all the jungles, the rivers, all the universes.

— *Is that what you feel when you write?*

— There comes a moment when you're writing and you feel tired and you keep going out of discipline, but at a certain point, not knowing why, you connect with something pleasurable, like a source of energy, and then time flows quickly. I think that is the creative moment when man connects with his fellows.

Life has this very important symbolic character for me, because we are symbols, we're not simply human beings.

— You're very fond of water as a symbol.

— Perhaps because I always have it here before my eyes, whether I'm working or resting, this magnificent Atlantic Ocean, and this superb Copacabana beach. Water is one of the most symbolic things, being one of the basic elements of life and creation. Look, in the sea there is a moment of conflict when swells are formed. That's the moment when we distinguish the sea from the land. And that zone, sometimes calm, sometimes turbulent, sometimes fatal, is where creation happens.

I have great respect for the mystery of things. I know there are things that happen, but we don't know why and we have to respect that dark, mysterious zone.

— Sometimes you begin to write something and later regret it and abandon or destroy it.

— That's true. When I start to write, I don't know if I'm doing well or badly. I write first of all for myself, since I am my first reader.

I used to be in the habit of giving my books to others to read before I published them. Not any more. I carry the responsibility. And when I realize I'm writing something that's not working, I abandon it. It happened to me not long ago with a book I was writing about gypsies. At a certain point I gave up on it.

— *And how do you become aware that something you're writing isn't working?*

— Because I notice it's not sincere, it doesn't flow. You feel it inside.

— *How do you choose the subjects you write about?*

— I am a writer who's politically committed to the times in which we live, and my great search has always been the spiritual one. That's why this question is always present in my books. There was a time when I thought I could answer everything I was asked, but now I realize that's not possible, as well as it being ridiculous. There could be explanations for everything, taken from masters and gurus. But they wouldn't be mine. The truth is we continue to be a mystery and I'm only sure of one thing, and that is that we have to give the best of ourselves. And that's when you feel content. If you don't act sincerely in your life you deceive yourself and you deceive others, but not for long, because the empire of evil has its own logic too.

– *What is the creative process like that leads to a new book?*

– I'll give you a graphic example. I have just returned from Japan, where I spent several days signing books. I saw a curious artefact for scaring deer there that made me think of my literary process. The artefact in question was a piece of bamboo with a hole in it, which gradually fills with water. When the bamboo fills up completely, the water comes out and hits something making a loud noise that scares the deer away. That was a symbol for me because we fill up and, at a certain point, feel the need to share. We could call it love or the need to participate in life, but the truth is when we do something with enthusiasm, we do it because we're driven by the need to share.

– *And you, personally, how do you fill up?*

– I fill up unthinkingly, in the classic process of pregnancy, after having made love with life, although I never know who the father is. For two years, in the interval between one book and the next, I do nothing, I don't take notes, but I am totally available to life. And, at some point, something gets inside me and weighs me down. And soon I feel the need to write.

– *And how do you know when you're ready to 'give birth'?*

– I notice because I start to feel, I wouldn't say angry, but irritable. That's when I say to myself, 'I feel full, heavy, ready to give birth.'

– So, in other words, you have to be open to receive and then you have to get some fresh air to manifest it.

– That is precisely the classic alchemic formula, summed up in dissolving and coagulating. So, then you have to dissolve and concentrate. It's like the heart's mechanism, and so many others in nature.

– Is it important for you to have disciplined hours for writing or do you prefer anarchy?

– I like anarchy in other things, but when it comes to writing, discipline is essential for me. Discipline is the most positive thing I got from my education at the Jesuit school, which was so negative in other respects. For me, in general, when I sit in front of the computer ready to start a book, a terrible laziness takes hold of me. I say to myself, 'But I've written enough books already, I'm an established writer, why do I need more.' Of course, this is just an excuse for my laziness. Beginning is always difficult. Later it starts to flow, but the hard thing is when you find yourself halfway through a book, because you don't have the enthusiasm you had when you began and you know you're still far from finishing. That's where so many writers succumb.

— *Do you, like some writers, have habits or superstitions you always follow when the time comes to write?*

— Oh yes, many. One of them is that when I start a book I cannot stop even for one day because if I do I won't be able to start again. Sometimes, to keep from stopping, when I'm travelling, I write on aeroplanes and in hotels. Except I broke that chain with my book, *Veronika Decides to Die*. At first I was faithful, but then I had to leave it for a time. Thank God I was able to keep going, which shows that even in superstitions there are exceptions to the rule. Another of my habits is that I have to write my books here in Brazil, in my house in Copacabana.

— *But strangely, almost all your books draw inspiration from Spain and none, so far, from Brazil.*

— Exactly. That's another of my paradoxes. My passion for Spain arises from the fact that when I was very little I had a Spanish nanny. Since then all my fantasies and my imagination have been directed towards that country. That's why I have so many works set in Spain. But in order to write I need a certain distance, and to be here, despite getting involved in thousands of problems. But I need the routine of daily life to create. And I also feel profoundly Brazilian and that's why I need my Brazil to write.

— What does being Brazilian mean to you?

— It means living in a permanent breeding ground, in a mixture of races unique in the world, with African, indigenous Brazilian, Japanese, European influences. It's that mix of a thousand things that's taught us Brazilians to be tolerant with the spiritual world, with all the magic that manifests through the basic symbols of music, dance and poetry.

— In Europe that tolerance no longer exists.

— It's not that it doesn't exist, it's that you've forgotten it. Let's think about history for a minute: when the nomads began to come down from the mountains to build the first cities, who chose the places, and what motives led them to favour one specific place to raise their city? They weren't logical criteria, but magical, extraordinary ones. It was a time when God, who didn't yet have a name, because he wasn't in a specific place, walked along with men on their continuous wanderings. Polytheism and names for God were born with the creation of the city.

— And they started to build temples.

– Cities began when people discovered agriculture and understood they could feed themselves without having to be constantly on the move. And also understood the slow process of time between sowing the seed and harvesting the fruits. That's precisely my mental journey as a writer. It's when man began to discover the relationship between love and pregnancy. That's why, when that process was unknown, no one knew who the father was. Then, man began to notice it takes time for things to germinate, to be born and grow.

– And cities grew up around the temples.

– The first wall they constructed was not the one that enclosed the city but the one they raised around the temple. Thus the sacerdotal caste arose, the power of the sacred. God will have a name by then, and an altar and a part of the population will take it over. That's how the separation between the sacred – the temple, where power resides – and the profane, which is the world beyond that wall, gets created.

– And that division has lasted until now.

– The structure of the city changes, means of transport, social systems and government all change, but the symbol of that wall, the separation between the sacred and the profane, remains in place. A separation Jesus breaks in the Gospels. He tells the Samaritan woman that a day will come when men will no longer worship in this temple or in another but 'in the spirit and in truth'. And in the parable of the good Samaritan, he praises the generous conduct of the Samaritan who helps the wounded man fallen by the roadside, despite the fact that Samaritans were atheists, without religion, while he criticizes the Levite, who was the man of the sacred, the man of the temple.

But now, many people are starting to realize that to enjoy mystery and inject it into our daily lives, it's necessary to break down that separation between the sacred and the profane. Once we break down that wall, the sacred starts to penetrate the profane. And that's what happens in Brazil.

– That is precisely the big difference Europeans notice when coming into contact with Brazilians.

– And do you know why? Because in Brazil, with its confusion of races and cultures, there wasn't time to build up that wall around the altar. African slaves arrived in Bahía with their rituals and got together with Christians, and syncretism was born. It isn't always positive but it's better than one religion wanting to dominate the rest. Since that wall separating the sacred from the profane didn't get built, mystery, the magic of reality, penetrated everywhere. The sacred entered into the profane.

That's why Brazilians aren't allergic to the spirit and accept all experiences impregnated with spirituality or mystery. I don't know if you've noticed that the only football players in the World Cup who come onto the ground holding hands to transmit energy, are those of the Brazilian national team. Ronaldo is always at the end of the line and he has to have one hand free to touch the ground and collect the energy of the pitch.

— So Brazilians are not only tolerant of all religious and spiritual manifestations, but it forms part of their lives at all levels.

— If you come here for New Year's Eve, to Copacabana beach in Río, you'll see an incredible spectacle. You'll find yourself among a million people, all of them Catholics, but who come down to the seaside, dressed entirely in white to throw flowers into the water, which is an African ritual. Here all beliefs coexist, and believers know how to reconcile them without troubling their consciences, as theologians know all too well.

That's why I say being Brazilian greatly influences my artistic creative process, because here people are very intuitive, not ashamed of experimenting with the spiritual or the magical, they are much more paradoxical than Cartesian. They are tremendously human and open to all that is mysterious.

— That's why you've chosen to live here.

— I've chosen to live in Brazil and specifically in this city, Río de Janeiro, which is the most marvellously transgressive and lively city in the world. I've already told you I am a man of extremes. William Blake wrote: 'The road of excess leads to the palace of wisdom.' That's what I believe. So, when I write a book, I would say I write *'a la brasileña'*, that is, passionately. And so, within Río, I've chosen to live here in Copacabana, facing the sea. In Río there are quieter places, in the middle of the woods, but this is a place of strong contrasts, between the sea and the forest. You see how the pavement by the beach is black and white, and here misery and wealth live shoulder to shoulder. There are other hybrid neighbourhoods. This is a neighbourhood with a strong personality, where my spirit feels at home to write.

— *Speaking of New Year's Eve, do you spend it here, in Río?*

— No, you're going to think it strange, but I spend the last night of the year in the grotto of Lourdes.

— *You spend New Year's Eve in Lourdes? They say that for the last night of last century there wasn't a single hotel room or restaurant place in any of the world's important cities.*

— Well, there was a corner for me in that grotto. In 1989 I spent my birthday there alone, and it was a very intense experience.

And, the following year Cristina and I started spending New Year's Eve in the grotto of the apparitions. It is usually very cold. There are never more than fifty people. The first time, I found it very moving, I was almost spellbound by the Virgin. It is religion as worship, as adoration. The people there, from very different places, with very different emotions, feel united merely by the religious atmosphere of simple prayer.

— And how do you celebrate the New Year?

— In a practical sense, we don't. There's no joy or sadness, just serenity. It almost always rains. We usually dine first in the hotel, a simple meal, and then we wish each other a Happy New Year. You experience the mystery of faith up close. There was one year when I went to the grotto in the morning and there was a man sitting there meditating. And when I came back in the evening he was still there. Perhaps he was fulfilling a promise, I don't know. The truth is that everything is very magical that night in Lourdes, with so few people.

— But don't you think the magical dimension is a little out of fashion in a society that gives priority to production, consumption, technology and the globalization of the market?

– I'm going to tell you something, Juan: to start with, all that about the globalization of the market, the stock exchanges, and so on, is the most magical thing in existence. That is real magic. Because don't tell me that today's economists know anything about it. They're lost. They're incapable of making a prediction, of planning anything, because the magic of the international markets, the stock exchanges, comes along and it's enough for the Japanese economy to get a cold and they all catch fatal flu. They put up with all these magical effects they don't understand and cannot control.

All these economic gurus, these high priests, have their religion, their dogma, their mysteries, their secrets they play with to impress poor mortals, but reality is that today the magic of the stock markets is leaving them naked, without religion.

– *But you play the market too.*

– Very little. And I've always challenged and disconcerted the broker. I go and tell him, 'These falling stocks are going to go back up.' He says 'No' and I say 'Yes'. And when they go up, he asks me, 'But how did you know?' And I answer him, 'Because I have feminine intuition, and if they've fallen so far, it stands to reason that they're going to go back up. You say it's not possible and give me a thousand reasons, and I'm guided simply by the movement of the tides, where if the tide is low that's because it's got to come back in later.' It's that simple.

– *It's a magic that's getting harder and harder for them to control.*

– They just make scientific conjectures, we believe they know, but the truth is they're completely in the dark, like all those economists. It's like the forces of good and evil. If one day the forces of evil decide to devaluate Brazil's currency, and ruin our economy, they will do it and there's no economist who can do anything about it, no government capable of stopping it. That's why I very rarely get involved in those things, I put my money in savings accounts and that's that.

– *Do you believe in evil then?*

– Good question. I believe in two evils: natural and artificial. Natural evil, because I am a monotheist, is God's left hand, things that happen. Artificial evil is things we do and project in time, because this is a symbolic universe that transforms in reality. To put an end to darkness, it is enough to turn on a light, because you can't light the darkness.

– *Then you say you don't like metaphors.*

– There are things you can only explain with images. But getting back to evil, what we call evil, are things that just happen, which one can't understand and that wound. The classic example is Job.

— Don't you believe there's a danger we'll end up justifying pain and injustice, instead of combating the structures that produce them?

— That's always a danger and it's the danger of the spiritual quest in general. We always have to be alert. But I assure you I've never known anyone, not a single person who seriously follows their spiritual path, who justifies suffering and doesn't do anything to combat it within their capabilities.

— But, don't you believe there are people who boast of being very spiritual and who do nothing to change this unjust world?

— I don't think you should generalize. Who changed my life, for example? They were people who illuminated me with their example, and so they had to be visible people and not have complexes about showing their virtue. In the Gospels it says you don't light a lamp to put it behind a door but to light up the house.

I have also seen horrible things in my life, people who have tried to manipulate me in the world of magic and in the spiritual world, and I have to admit that, in the seventies, even I tried to manipulate people. But in the end, people aren't as stupid as we think and they know how to distinguish between those who lead them towards the light and those who lead them towards the darkness. Just a few days ago I saw a television programme about sects. I have a horror of sects, but the way they directed that programme was pitiful. They think we're all small children unable to think for ourselves.

— Getting back to your condition as a writer, don't you feel responsible for what's happening? Because millions of people read your books, and not passively but actively.

— Our digression is also important for my readers to understand me better as a writer, because you write what you feel and experience. And as far as my responsibility goes, yes, I do feel responsibility, and quite a bit, precisely because I see the effects my books have. Because I am conscious of having been mistaken several times in my life.

I know I am a famous writer, translated the world over, much loved, but also pirated, detested and hated. But present and alive. I think the first question I ask myself as a writer is whether I'm being honest with myself. And up to this moment, I feel I have been. And also, having to travel the world, talking over and over again, in different places, about the same book obliges me to reflect on them. Especially because I have to launch the same books in different places at different times and that keeps me reflecting on them.

— Does it bother you that they see you as a guru or master as well as a writer?

— That is a problem. Sometimes that border between writer and guru bothers me, and I wonder if I am prepared for that challenge. It is a time bomb. I've managed to elude it so far, limiting myself to my position as writer. I act as a catalyst about what I have to say in my books.

— *That's exactly what Federico Fellini said, when asked for an opinion on something that happened or would happen, he protected himself by saying, 'I've already said it all in my films.'*

— That's wonderful. The truth is, up till now I've tried to defend myself so as not to emerge from my role as a writer. Five years ago, I could have spent my whole time giving lectures, courses, and so on, making lots of money. In Brazil I'd sold six million books, which meant many million readers. If they'd each paid just one dollar to come to one of my lectures, I'd be made of money. But I didn't do it.

— *How do you handle the criticisms some make of your way of writing?*

— Critics have their job and always help writers. I've never felt personally hurt by a review, for I am aware that I decided to write very simply, directly, so everyone can understand me. That's why some people say I don't know how to write or that I'm too simplistic in my writing. I don't think there is one correct way to write.

Every writer has their own personality and peculiarities, and each writes for his own audience.

But I never confront my critics, and when we meet I'm friendly to them, not out of cynicism or because I feel superior for selling millions of books, but because I've a very clear conscience about doing things the way I do them. I do feel a great love and affection for simple people who are sincere and real. I identify with them.

— However, I have seen you very angry with some publishers.

— And I'll explain why. At first I didn't have any experience and I signed my contracts language by language. And it so happened that my books arrived in India from another country at a price of fifteen dollars, when the average price of a book in India is around three dollars. And this is a country of five hundred million people. How can they send such expensive books from England or Ireland? So I confronted them. I demanded my books be published in each country, so they'd be priced in accordance with the place and not be imported luxury books. The same thing happened to me in Latin America and Africa. I objected because my Portuguese publisher sent my books to Africa at European prices. I told him, 'Mario, you're a socialist and you don't believe in God. I do believe, but your socialist heart has to understand that we can't sell books in Africa at such high prices. They have to be printed there.' And now we have books, in Angola for example, in popular editions.

— You keep your library hidden. Why?

— As I told you before, I don't like to be ostentatious about what I'm reading or have just read. In 1973 I had a whole apartment full of books. One day I came home to find all the shelves had fallen, and I thought if I'd been there I would have been killed, buried by books. I thought of Borges, when he wondered, in his library, 'Which of these books will I never read again?' I asked myself the same question. 'Why do I have all these books I know I'll never read again? Who am I trying to impress?' And I decided then my library would not exceed four hundred books, which is already a lot if I want to reread them. And I don't keep them here in the house, but somewhere else in a cupboard.

— Do you feel like a transgressor in your books?

— To be a writer, you need a little fantasy, a little transgression, you need to break the rules of conventional wisdom. I always try to reconcile rigour with compassion and so we have a minimum of wisdom so as not to commit certain stupidities. But what we can't do is kill the child within. I think my books are read much more by the child we all carry inside us. That's why I write stories I like, that's why I don't write philosophical disquisitions or grand, boring theories. If someone wants to know what I think of life and things, then I'll talk to you, like I'm doing with this book, but if I want to talk about the limits of madness and reality, then I'll write a novel with a plot I like and within the story will be all of that. But the story speaks to the child, the child is the commander who speaks to the brain and to the rest.

— *Someone could object that the search for the child within is the fear of encountering our adult side.*

— And what is that adult side? What is maturity? It is the beginning of decline, because when a fruit is ripe, you either eat it or it rots. Fear of the child who lives within us? How ridiculous! Who is the man who can say he is now mature, adult, who no longer needs to believe in God, and is a model for us all? Only a madman could say that. The truth is we're all evolving, maturing and being born at every moment.

— *It's like those who say they aren't afraid of anything.*

— That's just it. In one of my books a character asks, 'What is courage?' Courage is the fear that causes prayer. I believe in it very strongly, because if you don't have fear, you can't have courage either. That's the great paradox, because if I wasn't afraid, I'd throw myself out the window or let myself get hit by a car. A man with values is a man with fears who doesn't let himself be intimidated by them.

— *Who were your idols in your youth?*

— Essentially, a musician and a writer: John Lennon and Jorge Luis Borges. To try and meet the great Argentinian writer in person, I once took a bus from here in Río de Janeiro to Argentina. I was that fanatical about him. I managed to find out his address. I went with a girl. We arrived at the address I'd been given. They told me there that he was at a hotel across the street from his house. I approached him. He was sitting down. I had travelled forty-eight hours without sleeping to speak to him, but confronted with his presence, I went mute. I said to myself, 'I am in the presence of my idol and idols don't speak.' I didn't say a word to him. My girl-friend couldn't understand. I explained that, deep down, I just wanted to see my hero and I'd done it. Words were not necessary.

— *It's a very strong link, that's lasted your whole life.*

— Absolutely. Borges has been a great influence on my work. I adore his prose and his poetry. I'm proud to have been born on 24 August, like him, under the same sign, although, obviously, many years later.

— *Do you like his prose better than his poetry?*

– I love everything he's written. I've read his poems thousands of times, I know many of them off by heart.

– *That's a little hard to believe. Shall we test you?*

– Right now. Would you like me to recite one of his sonnets for you?

– *Let's hear it.*

– Listen to this, for example:

I will not be happy now. It may not matter.
There are so many more things in the world.
Any random instant is as crowded
and varied as the sea. A life is brief,
and though the hours seem long, there is another
dark mystery that lies in wait for us
* – death, that other sea, that other arrow*
that frees us from the sun, the moon, and love.
The happiness you gave me once and later
took back from me will be obliterated.
That which was everything must turn to nothing.
I only keep the taste of my own sadness
and a vain urge that turns me to the Southside,
to a certain corner there, a certain door.

(Coelho recited the poem without a single mistake, without hesitation, in perfect Spanish. The poem is a sonnet called '1964 (II)', [here in Alastair Reid's translation]. He passed the test with flying colours.)

— *Where would you like to see your books placed in bookshops?*

— Some in the Literature section, others in Philosophy, but not in Esoteric. And I say this unashamedly, not modestly, but with pride.

— *And how are you as a reader?*

— I have an almost magical relationship with books, and here too I have my superstitions. First of all, I only read books I buy, never those I'm given. I receive about twenty books a day and I don't even open them.

— *But you could be missing something marvellous, just because it's a gift.*

— If it's something really good, I'll find out about it and then go to a bookshop and buy it. I don't think writers should give away their books. Shoe factories never send me pairs of shoes, why do people have to send me books?

— Don't tell me you never make exceptions. On occasion you've given books of yours away and on others you've read books that you were sent. You showed me a letter, for example, from the Brazilian Minister of the Armed Forces thanking you for sending him a copy of Manual of the Warrior of the Light, *which he liked very much.*

– Of course I make exceptions. In that case it was the minister himself who asked me for it, if he hadn't, I wouldn't have given it to him.

— And have you not read my book of conversations with José Saramago, Possible Love, *which I sent you?*

– I did read it, and not just once. But that's something else. You were coming here to do a book with me like the one you did with him, and I had a tremendous curiosity to know what a famous and successful writer like Saramago is really like, and naturally I wanted to read it. The same goes for your book *A God for the Pope*. I didn't even know it was in the bookshops. They told me about it in Madrid and so I asked you for a copy, because I'm very interested to know the psychology of Pope John Paul II. But in general, when I want a book, even if only out of respect for the author, I don't want to be given it, I want to buy it.

— But the foundation sometimes buys books in your name to give away.

– That's true, the foundation bought twelve thousand of my books to send to libraries in prisons, hospitals and such like. The publisher asked me if I wanted them at cost, and I said I wanted to pay full price, as if they'd been sold by a bookshop.

(One of his nieces was involved in this conversation. Coelho confessed he'd once given her a copy of one of his books and he asked her, 'Have you read it?' And his niece answered that she hadn't. Her uncle pretended to be angry with her, 'What? You've got an uncle who's read the world over and you don't even read his books? If you'd bought it with your own money, I bet you would have read it.' My partner, affectionately teasing Coelho, gave him a book of her poetry and said, 'I'm giving you this so you can throw it in the bin.' Coelho, smiled, hugged her and said, 'You'll have to sign it for me.')

– *How much of you is in your books?*

– In reality I am all the characters in my books. The only person I'm not is the alchemist.

– *And why is that?*

– Because the alchemist already knows everything, while I know I don't know everything, there's lots I don't know. Of course, in *The Alchemist* I'm the shepherd, the crystal merchant and even Fatima.

In the other books I'm always the main character. I am even Brida. In two books I'm completely myself: in *The Valkyries* and *The Pilgrimage*. The fact is, the majority of my books, although they're literary narratives, are not fiction. They are actual things I've experienced. The same holds true with *Veronika Decides to Die*. It's nothing more than the fictionalized experience of the terrible story I told you, of the three times I was committed to an asylum.

– *Do you feel like a pilgrim writer?*

– All writers need to be in motion, at least internally. I don't think Proust moved much physically but he was widely travelled just the same. All the great classics of literature are stories of great journeys, from the Bible to the *Divine Comedy*, from *Don Quixote* to the *Iliad*. It's always the search for Ithaca, it's the metaphor of birth and death, that great journey we all have to make, whether we want to or not.

CHAPTER X

Readers

❧

'Above all, my readers are my accomplices.'

'I write for the child we have inside.'

❧

Paulo Coelho has millions of readers on every continent and in every language. His readership is difficult to profile given its remarkable diversity. Although he receives thousands of letters and messages, that is still not enough to really know what those readers are actually like. What can be known is how he sees himself vis-à-vis those millions of readers with whom he feels himself to be more of a friend than master and, above all, an accomplice. He's able to perceive a small sample of his readers' feelings towards him on his world tours. And what he feels is the degree of enthusiasm that not just his books but his very presence evokes. And his store of tales includes moving, even magical and surprising scenes.

— Let's talk about the profile of your readers.

— What I want to tell you first of all is that my relationship with that enormous mass of anonymous readers is a very intense one, it's not a master–disciple relationship or a typical relationship between a writer and his readers.

— What kind of relationship is it then?

— It's a friendship, even though we don't know each other, as though I shared something very personal with them, but something of mine that is everyone's and that is the best of each of us.

– Let's see the last letter you received.

– Look, this is very strange. It's from a young man who's sent me a photograph with both of us in it. You can see we were at some book launch in England. It is a very feminine letter with drawings. He says he's studying Portuguese, and dreams of angels. He's sent me the photo so I can sign it for him. I don't remember it at all, but he tells me where we met and how he felt. He also talks about *The Alchemist*.

I receive thousands of letters like this one, sometimes eight or ten pages long. But I've already told you, with few exceptions, the ones who write are simple readers, because important people tend not to.

– Do you think more men read you than women?

– At first, many more women. Now, the tendency has changed. When I started giving readings, ninety per cent of the audience was female, and ten per cent male. Now the proportion is about sixty per cent women and forty per cent men. They aren't so frightened of showing their emotions anymore, and line up to get their books signed, just like the women. And I imagine that must be the proportion of readers too. But the truth is, I don't know exactly.

– Have you been surprised sometimes?

– Oh yes, many times. Sometimes I meet people who I couldn't imagine were readers of mine. Then I think my readers belong to a very multi-coloured universe. What I do see is that their relationship to me is very strong. It doesn't make much difference whether you write well or badly, it's almost a brotherhood, a complicity. More than readers, they're often my accomplices.

When I think about my readers sometimes, that they leave their houses, take a bus, go to a bookshop, and probably have to wait to buy one of my books because it's full, it's something that really moves me.

– *Why do you think you have so much success with readers?*

– I think when people read one of my books say, 'I could have written this book, he's talking about things I know, but had forgotten,' it's what we mean by the collective unconscious. I think my books are connected to a mysterious creative process that has much of the feminine in it.

– *What is that feminine side?*

– It's that part, as we said before, that doesn't erect a wall between the sacred and the profane, that knows how to use intuition and the magical dimension of existence and applies paradox to daily life.

— Do you think you represent for young people today what Castaneda did for those of '68?

— In *The Pilgrimage*, my first book, I mention Castaneda in the prologue and identify Petrus with Don Juan, but I don't feel like a continuation of him. Precisely because on the Santiago pilgrimage I learned the most important lesson of my life: that the extraordinary is not the birthright of a chosen and privileged few, but of all people, even the humblest. That is my one certainty: we are all the manifestation of the divinity of God. In Castaneda, on the contrary, only the chosen are able to penetrate mystery. But Castaneda is still one of my idols. He changed my life. When he died in April 1998, I dedicated my *O Globo* column to him.

— As far as I can see, the pilgrimage to Santiago was very important to your future life.

— Oh yes. It was a radical experience for me. When I started, I also thought that finding your destiny, being able to penetrate the mysteries of the spirit, were things reserved for the chosen few. But half way along, I suffered a deep crisis.

— There are those who doubt you actually did it, and for so many days.

– I know. But they haven't read my book about that experience; if they had they wouldn't say it. It would be impossible to write the way I wrote about it, with all sorts of details, almost day-by-day, without having done it. And it would be especially impossible for it to have provoked such a turnaround in my life if I hadn't taken it seriously.

– *You stayed in Madrid afterwards.*

– For several months. Every time there were bullfights, I went to watch. They were happy months for me because I wasn't doing anything and no longer had that idea of the elect, I didn't think pain was sacred anymore, or wisdom complicated, or good taste sophisticated. And I no longer had the stupid idea that the more difficult things were, the more important they were.

– *The pilgrimage to Santiago threw everything into confusion for you.*

– And I want my readers to know just how true that is. That experience put me in contact with common people who I realized were full of wisdom and this shattered all my preconceived notions. For example, I'll never forget my meeting with a young lad in a bar in a small village one day. He was ignorant, he certainly wouldn't have known who Proust was, but he told me such fantastic things about life, he left me astonished. Another didn't open his mouth but offered me a helpful gesture of affection such as I would never have done in my life despite all my religion, knowledge and searching.

— *And you came back changed.*

— It was a radical change, one hundred and eighty degrees. And it was in that moment when I took on the duty of writing about those things, for those common people we assume to be ignorant, and who possess an incredible hidden wisdom. I considered myself a writer, but I'd never decided to write. The great lesson of that pilgrimage was coming to understand that beauty is in simplicity. That's why I told you that my house, as you can observe, is as simple as possible. It's almost empty. Only there, at the back of the living room, there's a flower. And it's beautiful because there's nothing else. Simplicity is the greatest of beauties.

— *Speaking of common people, did you know that the Catholic theologians wouldn't accept the truth of the apparitions of the Virgin for a very strange reason, that if the Virgin had something to say to humanity she wouldn't use such simple and ignorant girls like the seers Lourdes and Fatima?*

— As if Jesus Christ himself had been a great wise man in his day. He wasn't. And he didn't surround himself with wise men but with ignorant fishermen to help him spread his message of truth.

There's an interesting science fiction novel called *The Black Cloud*. It tells of a cloud that came and, with its knowledge, consumed universes and galaxies. The cloud was total knowledge, and it was going to consume the Earth too. Man managed to communicate with the cloud and tell it there was intelligent life on Earth, that it should go somewhere else. But the men said to it, 'Before you go, pass all your knowledge to Earth, since you're so smart. Choose the most intelligent man and connect to him.' The black cloud connected to the wise man, who, upon contact suffered a massive cerebral haemorrhage. But when he was in hospital, before he died, a person came in to clean the room and the man said the cloud had made a mistake, that it should have chosen him.

– *Why?*

– Very simple, because the wise man already had his universe constructed in his head, and when the cloud's knowledge came, it caused so many problems it destroyed him; however the other man, with his simplicity, his common intelligence, without prejudices, would have received it without contradictions and contentedly. *The Black Cloud* by Fred Hoyle is a science-fiction classic. And it fits perfectly with what I was just telling you about the readers I write for. I write for the child we all have inside. There is a false mysticism about children and innocence, as if innocence made people stupid. No, there is the innocence of enthusiasm, of surprise, of adventure. And that is felt most of all by children. That's what Jesus meant when he said in the Gospels that he was going to teach his wisdom to children and hide it from the wise and powerful. All this is very important in the philosophy of my books.

— You said in your meetings with your readers around the world that mysterious, even magical things, happen.

— It's true. And it's a good thing I've got live witnesses, because otherwise, no one would believe it. I'll tell you a couple of those stories. One time I was giving a lecture at a bookshop in Miami called Books & Books, about *Beside the River Piedra I Sat Down and Wept* in which the main character is a woman called Pilar. At one point in the lecture I said, 'Gustave Flaubert once said, "I am Madame Bovary." And I would like to add, "I am Pilar."' As always in my American lectures, I read a few paragraphs from the book and then took questions from the audience. While I was reading, we heard a loud noise, as if something had fallen. But I kept reading without stopping. When I finished I said out loud, 'Now, let's find out what happened.' It was a book that had fallen off a shelf. I picked it up and couldn't believe it: it was *Madame Bovary* by Gustave Flaubert. I took that book with me. I have it here. The people were astonished. Things like this happen to me often. It's strange that of the thousands of books there, the very one I'd mentioned in my lecture would fall off a shelf. You can ask Michael Kaplan, the owner of the bookshop to confirm it, he was the most surprised of all.

— What was the other story you wanted to tell?

— That happened in Miami too, a city I don't like at all. I was doing a tour of the United States and from there I had to go to Japan. I wasn't yet used to those international tours, and I did them the way publishers organized them. Now I plan them. I travel for a month and then, if I can, I rest for a month: if not, it's exhausting

Normally the editor doesn't come with you for the whole tour, they usually send someone who has nothing to do with the editor.

— Who was with you in Miami?

— Harper's Miami representative. I was going to do a reading at a bookshop, we were on our way there. It was around eight o'clock in the evening. She said to me, 'Wait, I'm just going to kiss my boyfriend goodbye and I'll be right back.' I sat by myself waiting. The United States is a difficult country and I was tired from travelling so much. I felt angry there, sad, lonely, bitter. I sat there in the middle of Miami and said to myself, 'What am I doing here? I don't need to do all this, my books sell just fine on their own.

I miss Brazil, I'm homesick.' And I lit up a cigarette and thought, 'That bitch just leaves me here on my own and goes off to kiss her boyfriend.'

– And, I imagine, at that moment something unusual happened to you.

– It so happened that three people walked past me with a twelve year-old girl. The girl turned to one of the people and said, 'Have you read *The Alchemist?*' I froze. The woman, who must've been the girl's mother, said something I didn't catch and the girl insisted, 'You have to read that book, it's really good.' I couldn't just sit there any longer so I stood up and said, 'I'm the author of *The Alchemist.*' The girl's mother looked at me and said, 'Come on, let's get out of here, he's crazy.' Then I went to call the girl from the publisher who had gone to kiss her boyfriend to come over and tell them I wasn't crazy, that I really was the author of the book.

We did manage to catch up with them, though they'd run off. The girl told them, 'I'm American and this gentleman is not a madman, he really is the author of *The Alchemist.*' Then the little girl said very happily, 'I believed you, but they didn't.' My escort said to her, 'This is a great lesson for you. Follow your intuition, mothers aren't always right.'

I invited the three people to the reading. I introduced the little girl, told the whole story and asked for a round of applause for them.

This is what we mean when we talk about omens. One minute my energy level was an inch above ground, unenthusiastic, empty, then that child brought me a message from heaven, an angel made use of her to cheer me up and convince me of the importance of meeting my readers in person.

— How do you answer those who say you can't be a good writer because such simple people are so enthused by your books?

— I say that's cultural fascism. Some of those intellectuals, their mouths full of democracy, deep down they're convinced the people are idiots.

— You are a loved and hated author. What does love mean to you?

— It's a kind of magic, a nuclear force that can help you realize your self or destroy you. For me, love is at the same time the most productive and most destructive force in the world.

It's difficult to find real critics who analyse Coelho's works and especially those who understand that Paulo Coelho is more than just a writer. He is also a social and cultural phenomenon that deserves to be studied. Sometimes his Spanish readers ask me what they say about him in Brazil, about his books, about the phenomenon he represents. And so, when the time came to publish this book, I was looking for a review that didn't go over the top in its praise, or verge on the ridiculous, such as one critic who, when asked for his opinion of the works of Coelho, answered: 'I haven't read them and I don't like them.'

I found an article that impartially analyses the phenomenon in all its breadth. It is entitled 'Why Paulo Coelho?' by the well-known writer and journalist Carlos Heitor Cony, published in the magazine *República*, in May, 1999. He says:

'In Paris during the Book Fair, I witnessed in person the literary and publishing phenomenon of our time. Paulo Coelho has gained a degree of international respect and popularity never before known in Brazilian cultural life.

'There are many who turn up their noses at him, not just because of his success but because they consider his literature to be minor, mercantile and definitely sub-literary.

'That is not how I view it. I am not a personal friend of the writer; we are polite, even warm to each other, but we never exchange more than fifty words when we meet. But for a long time now I've had an explanation for his success. Here it is.

'The century that is ending began with two utopias which seemed to be about to solve all the problems of body and mind. Marx and Freud, each, in his so-called scientific field, established rules that affected millions of human beings, concerned with either social justice or justice towards themselves, by way of psychoanalysis.

'It so happens that the century is ending and the two giant, powerful totems crumbled: they had feet of clay. Marx couldn't weather the failure of the regimes installed in his name, although socialism itself remains a possible dream which humanity hopes for. Freud was already challenged in his lifetime: fragmented, his followers proclaimed schisms and open rebellions. His original works survive as literature, but with ever-decreasing scientific value.

'From the collapse of these two utopias arose an emptiness in the human soul at the fin de siècle. And, as often happens, the call to mysticism, even magic, was going to be inevitable. And that's where our magus comes in, with his simplicity, sometimes resembling the age-old saints of all religions, pronouncing the necessary words, those everyone wants to hear, because, at a certain moment, they are within each of our souls.

'Paulo Coelho found those words in sacred and profane books, in oriental legends and occidental epics; he concocted a genial mixture of gospels, medieval magic books, charming and little-known oriental poetry. And he found the simplicity of one who doesn't want to impose anything, letting what he thinks and feels flow.

'Many tried and still try to do the same, but have not met with his success. For my own part, in professional and personal life, I tend rather towards an atrocious pessimism, a negative, cruel vision of human existence, finding myself on precisely the opposite end of the scale. But I am moved and feel the need to congratulate all those who, like Paulo Coelho, try, in their way, to improve mankind and make life less unbearable.'

Carlos Heitor Cony is a journalist, writer and author of more than twenty books, among them the novels *Almost Memory* and *The Tragic Poet's House*.

Then there's opinion of Nélida Piñon, ex-president of the Brazilian Academy of Letters.

The people who are hardest on Paulo Coelho are usually literary critics, who have gone so far as to accuse him of not knowing how to write. So we wanted to interview one of the great Brazilian writers, Nélida Piñon, whose works have been translated into all the principal languages, on her opinion of Paulo Coelho. Nélida was, until last year, president of the Brazilian Academy of Letters and her intellectual prestige is indisputable.

To my question about Paulo Coelho, with whom she participated in a round-table discussion in Barcelona during the *Liber* 1998 book fair, she answered:

'I don't have aesthetic prejudices. Coelho and I are part of the same scene, although we play different roles. He is a writer who honours my country with his writing and brings us honour from abroad. He is a very worthy person towards whom I profess a great appreciation. We met in a petrol station filling up our cars. When he saw me he greeted me with respect and a certain shyness. And I said, "Paulo, let's go out for a meal." That's how we met. And I'm going to tell you a secret: we even have plans to write a book together. We even have the title planned, but you'll forgive me if I don't reveal it yet.'

CHAPTER XI

Paula, Ana and María

❦

'I look at life, using the metaphor of the journey,
as a caravan: I know neither whence it
came nor where it's going.'

❦

Many of Coelho's readers have dreamt of sitting down with him in his house in Río de Janeiro and asking a thousand questions about his books and being able to exchange opinions with him.

That dream came true for three Spanish university students: Paula and Ana Gómez, two sisters, studying Architecture and Psychology, respectively, and María Chamorro, a friend of theirs who's studying to be a teacher.

I met the three of them on the aeroplane that took me from Madrid to Río de Janeiro, where I was going to do this book with Coelho. Curiously, all three were reading books by the Brazilian writer on the aeroplane: *Brida*, *The Fifth Mountain* and *By the River Piedra I Sat Down and Wept*. They told me how much they would love to have a chance to meet and speak with the author they so admired. And that's how this last chapter came about, when the three of them met Coelho in his house in Río. It was an encounter that lasted into the small hours of the morning and involved, as well as the three young students, the writer's wife Cristina, and the advertising executive, Mauro Salles, a great friend of Coelho's, who is also a poet and nationally esteemed man of culture.

The writer confided to us afterwards that no young people had ever questioned him so deeply and matter-of-factly.

Paula, a student of Architecture, admired the changes the writer had made to his apartment, how he had arranged the most important places for his personal life – the bedroom, his writing desk – in the most beautiful part of the house, overlooking the beach, leaving the back of the apartment, without a view, for the reception room.

Ana and María, as students of psychology and education, were thrilled to be able to have an informal dialogue with Coelho, without being weighed down by the age difference, although they were aware of the gap in experience and culture that there was between them. And they confessed they had grown personally from the encounter.

The three of them managed to connect with the writer because, as they said, 'It wasn't just an intellectual encounter, but a fundamentally vital one.'

P.G. – *We've been thinking about what to ask you and we've come up with two types of questions. Some to do with youth in general and other personal ones, from each of us.*

– Before you start, I want to make something clear: I don't want you to expect me to have an answer for everything. We're going to have a conversation between friends, because by talking we all learn from everyone, right?

P.G. – *We sometimes see young people in Spain – I don't know about Brazil – as quite despairing, not for the reasons we read in the paper or hear on the radio but something deeper, as if they didn't know which way to turn. Of course, that's not all young people, because I myself don't feel that way. What do you blame it on, you who know young people so well?*

– If you, Paula, don't feel despairing, how do you feel?

P.G. – *I feel something that has a lot to do with your books and it's something I'm finding out bit by bit. I think you get to a point when you discover yourself, you notice potential within yourself, that small encounters with the outside world start making you recognize. And that mix of authenticity and freedom makes me happy, allows me to make sense of my life. The question is, then, if what I think in connection with your books is true, why is it that sometimes when I pick up a book of yours it feels like a letter you've written to me.*

– All that, I think, has to do with the search for consciousness. I've talked a lot about it with Juan and Roseana, about how I came to be a writer. The key to my work, if we simplify it in the extreme, is what I call the personal story, like in *The Alchemist*. And although it seems mysterious to us, it's the reason for our existence. Sometimes it might not be clear and we strain against fate. That's when we feel weak and cowardly. But in the end our personal story is still there within us and we know why we're here. So, for me, the spiritual search is the search for total consciousness.

P.G. – *For a consciousness of oneself.*

– Yes, exactly. If you're drinking a glass of wine, you are illuminated because, while you drink it, you hear the sound of the countryside, where it came from, the family of the man who picked the grapes, what was around them ... the total consciousness of everything. That's what life gives to me. And you're concentrating on that, not in a sacrificial way, but joyfully, enthusiastically.

P.G. – *To feel yourself more yourself.*

– Exactly. That's why I'm thinking that throughout all these years a book is being written, though never physically manifest, which I call the 'Manual' and which would be a book of all the rules we have to follow, generation after generation. Sometimes we don't even know why we have to follow these rules but the rules are there and we keep crediting them. If on page twenty of that book it says: 'One must attend university at this time, one must earn a diploma, one must marry between the ages of twenty-five and thirty, ...' if you don't, you'll face a new conflict.

J.A. – *You're referring to the social system imposed on us.*

– To the social system as we know it today, imposed on generations, but since it's not a very clear or very visible book, we can combat it with clarity. All young people go through a stage, be it fighting intuitively against what is there and doesn't satisfy them, or accepting it. From the moment they accept it, they begin to live, not their life, but their parents' life, their family's, society's. Although I am an optimist, I believe when we reach total disillusionment, that is the moment of change, because you get to an extreme and stand back up with renewed strength.

J.A. – *Philosophically you're very Hegelian.*

– I am. I think what we seem to be seeing in young people, is that they've recognized the manual and they're going to change it. We are at this stage now, because sometimes the manual wins. The last generation tried to get around the manual by way of sports, the gym, the whole yuppie world. This generation seems different, I notice some evidence, I'm not sure exactly what, but I believe, for example, that the spiritual quest is one of the symptoms that there will be a very healthy revolution. I believe very strongly in the cleansing power of religion. I believe we are now reaching a point that will trigger the force of a sane revolution.

P.G. – *Regarding what you say about the manual, what has helped me take that step, get free of it, has been travelling.*

– Me too. Without doubt it was travelling that made me make the leap when I was your age.

M.C. – *I wonder if you're a believer in humanity. For example,* The Fifth Mountain, *is a biblical text and you develop a plot on top of it where you introduce your ideas; it's as if you were keeping a balance between the human and the spiritual. I don't know if it's because it's your style or because you want to reach everyone, you don't want to radicalize. Do you mean to say that only by having God close, can what you experience happen, or are you telling a little story so everyone can understand it, as if to say, God is humanity itself?*

– Principally, what you see in The Fifth Mountain isn't God, but the silence of God. It is the moment God doesn't speak, when God says, 'I'm going to help you but only once you make the decisions you have to make.'

M.C. – *Of course, it's what you were just saying, that if many things have happened to you in your life, it has more to do with trust than luck, because as soon as you begin to trust, you begin to see. Without trust your eyes are closed, and that's when you take a step and rush into a choice that you yourself wouldn't have made, when the omens begin and your life starts to have meaning.*

P.G. – *But it's trusting in something you don't know.*

– No, and you'll never know.

P.G. – *It's simply something that works. I've reached a moment – it wasn't the travelling itself but the journey has been the catalyst for many things – when I've been able to find something that frees me and makes me happy.*

– You know that the idea of the journey is in many of my books. Why? First of all, because I belong to the travelling generation, the hippy generation, that lived on the road, connecting with other cultures. And the journey has a very strong symbolic significance in people's lives. First, when you travel you're no longer yourself, you have to be open. If you ran into Juan Arias in a café and started talking, you'd think: this guy's trying to chat me up and things like that, but if you're travelling you're totally open because you know the experiences of the journey are not the monuments, museums or churches. I very rarely visit those places. I only do it if I really feel like it. Henry Miller put it very well when he said, one thing is them telling you Notre-Dame is fantastic, you've got to see it, and you go to Notre-Dame and yes, it is fantastic but you observe that you went there at the behest of others. However, if you'd turned a corner and found yourself staring at Notre-Dame, you'd have it all because you'd discovered it yourself. Often, the marvels of trips are tiny churches that aren't in the guidebooks, little nooks, whatever you find on your own. Those guidebooks terrify me sometimes.

J.A. – *Like what happened to us in Venice, we found the most incredible, tucked-away places and I'd been to Venice a thousand times, but always with guides. This time we said, 'Let's just get lost,' and we found unthinkable, marvellous little nooks, and wonderful scenes, like an old man who must've been about ninety, walking bent over down a lonely street. We could hear his footsteps and they were emblematic of a tired humanity sometimes abandoned to its fate.*

— That's it, the act of giving yourself over, trusting, because you're travelling, you know that what's going to connect you to the city, to things, is your individual experience, and secondly, the people. You're going to enjoy a country because the people there are nice, kind, helpful, or you'll detect the most beautiful thing there is, you know you have to be open to people and you open up, you're not protected by your environment anymore, you're a human being, with the essential human condition, which is solitude, although you're with a person, you're alone, just the same.

I have my friends here, I see them, I go to the beach, I walk along it, but there is a tendency to see the same people all the time, talk about the same things. But if I'm in Taiwan, I might say it's a horrible city, but in the end we went out to see it. And you talk to the first person who crosses your path, argue with the taxi driver, communicate with another ...

J.A. — *It's true, that's why they say travelling is the best university of life. You may have read tons of books about a city, but until you actually go you don't realize that all you've read hasn't been terribly useful.*

— Exactly. The other two things are that you leave your own environment, so you're not surrounded by familiarity; you're independent, you're lost, you need the help of others, this is also part of the human condition, letting yourself be led. Like in *The Alchemist*, though you might be on a journey, that journey depends on people who help you find your way, although your way is already written.

You have a relationship with the physical and with metaphysical world you don't understand so well. You don't understand the value of money, something so established and important in your life, something very metaphorical, because when you travel you don't know what's expensive and what's cheap anymore. Something might strike you as very expensive and really it's very cheap, or the opposite, you're always working it out.

The other thing is that you have to simplify your life to the utmost because you're not going to carry the weight of your vanity, so you try to make your luggage as light as possible. I'm always going from airport to airport and take a tiny suitcase. I know luggage is heavy and I realize I could live the rest of my life out of this tiny bag.

J.A. – *Roseana came to Madrid for three months and I was shocked when she showed up with just a carry-on bag.*

– And another thing you realize is that what you need for three months is what you need for three days, you can travel with the same bag. All the symbols of the journey start to reach very deep inside your psychology, that's why all religions, in one way or another, have pilgrimage and relieving yourself of the superfluous as important facets.

J.A. – *Another problem with journeys is you have to make an effort to under-stand languages you don't know.*

– It's similar to luggage. When you travel, you're obliged to sim-plify your life very much because after just a few days you won't have the vocabulary to speak to people. But having to simplify your language obliges you to start simplifying everything, includ-ing yourself. When I was twenty I travelled across the whole of the United States. I barely knew a word of English then, but at the end of the trip I felt clearer and simpler, because I didn't have words to discuss grand philosophical existential problems and had to reduce my language to the most elemental. And that takes great discipline.

M.C. – *And a journey is an upheaval, because the omens can be, in fact are, where you live. What probably happens is that travelling or something intense like that makes you see what you hadn't seen before, even though it was right in front of you.*

A.G. – *I wanted to raise the issue that in each person's individual story, you notice you're growing, but this growth often hurts. When I was little my legs hurt and the problem was they were growing and precisely that happens now, when I read your books, it hurts.*

– What's this? How do I hurt you?

A.G. – *Well, your books are a continuous confrontation with myself. And I see on the one hand I'm growing, but on the other, changing things hurts, because it's not just about putting things in, enriching me, but also about cleansing my soul of excess.*

– That's a very good definition. In his first book, Conan Doyle gives an extreme example: when Doctor Watson meets Sherlock Holmes, they're arguing about something everyone knows, something like that the Earth is round. Sherlock Holmes looks surprised and says, 'The Earth is round?' 'Of course!' says Watson, 'but didn't you know that?' 'No! I'd never thought about it, and I'm going to forget it as quickly as I can because my brain cannot contain it, there is very limited space!' So, I know the Earth is round, but since it's not going to help me very much in my life or my work, I'm going to forget about it quickly and register things more related to my work. Of course, it's not just a matter of adding but of taking away as well, taking away things that are there due to a very unconscious process: the manual, as we were saying.

P.G. – *Talking about youth, we were just saying that there are people who find it very hard to read books that raise these issues, that make them question their lives or who they are. It is a very human fear. That is, it could cause me pain to advance, it might hurt to question who I am. I have friends who say that. We were talking about it the other day at dinner. Personally, I would prefer to realize I'm a disaster and keep searching, than say I'm not going to look, in case*

I find something I don't like. I have friends who are scared to read books that oblige them to look within themselves. That's why I wanted to ask you if you think everyone has the ability to skip the manual and why.

– Let me tell you something that happened to me on the pilgrimage to Rome, also known as the feminine way. When I started walking, after a week or maybe ten days, I started to see my worst side, the most horrible; I saw myself as materialistic, vengeful, all the worst sentiments. So I went to speak with the guide and told her, 'Here I am, walking a sacred route, giving the best of myself, and instead of changing for the better, I'm changing into a small-minded, mean person.' She said, 'No, no, that's now, later the light will come, you're seeing how you really are right now, you haven't changed to feel that. You've started to see much more clearly the smallness of your world and that always makes things very clear.'

Because if we turn on lights we see spiders, evil, and then we turn them off, because we don't want to see cockroaches. We go through that process of painful growth, because the first thing we see is not the best, but the darkest part of ourselves, then comes the light.

M.C. – *I've noticed that you have to like yourself even with those little things we think are bad, because when you say to yourself, 'I'm so bad,' you start to see how small-minded and silly you are.*

That's why it bothers me when a small child has an accident and throws a glass onto the floor, people say, 'Isn't he cute! How funny!' But if you drop a glass on the floor they say, 'You idiot!'

The fact is we don't love ourselves, and when you say, 'I'm so bad,' it's because you don't love yourself; you have to like yourself even in your meanness. So I think it's not just about changing, but of recognizing that I'm small, fragile, but I have to love myself anyway and people have to accept me the way I am.

– I'll tell you something else. I don't see it quite that way. To my mind, it's all movement, which is why change is always happening. However, what paralyses us is guilt. You see things and you get paralysed by guilt, you don't feel worthy. I myself, the first thing I did here was say, 'What a son of a bitch I am!' so you wouldn't think you're here with some wise man who has all the answers, but just a normal person. I was helping myself by keeping you from creating a false image of me and so you would accept me from the beginning as I am. And without those stupid guilty feelings.

M.C. – *But the first thing is to love yourself and then not have fear of revealing yourself as you are. Because there are many pitfalls: that's not done, that's not said, you shouldn't say that, and so on.*

– Absolutely.

A.G. – *I think the basis for making the break is accepting you have rights, as a human being you have the possibility of seeing beyond the manual.*

– And that there is no sin. For example, that's why I think a lot, Catholic that I am, about Jesus Christ's first miracle. It wasn't a politically correct miracle. It wasn't curing a blind man or making a cripple walk. It was turning water into wine, a very mundane thing, very profane, simply because there wasn't any wine left. It wasn't something necessary to save humanity, no. At the wedding feast in Cana the wine ran out and Jesus asked, 'What should I do?' And he didn't doubt: I have the power to change water into wine so I'll do it. Not only that, but he turned it into a superb wine. For me, with this symbol, he meant: look, although I will go through moments of great pain, the way is the way of joy and not of pain. The inevitable is there, it awaits us, as in *The Fifth Mountain*, we can't avoid it, but we don't look for it either.

J.A. – *I think that's one of the errors some religions make, making sacrifice an end in itself. I always say that in the Gospels, each time Jesus Christ came across a pain, he took it away. He could have said: it suits you very well, keep it and you can sanctify yourself with it. No, he couldn't stand to see anyone suffer and he cured all illnesses, especially among the poor, who suffer the most.*

– I agree completely. All the pain I've had to confront in my life was pain I couldn't avoid, but I didn't look for it as a sacrifice. The word sacrifice comes from the sacred office, it has much more to do with the compromise you make towards whatever you're doing. There are times when you need to give something up so you can choose something else, but sacrifice as giving something up for its own sake has no meaning.

M.C. — *I don't think it's set out properly, the main thing isn't the sacrifice but the feeling of being loved, and that changes everything. I think that's why missionaries say it doesn't matter, they don't mind the sacrifice or the pain because they feel loved.*

J.A. — *But that's no longer a sacrifice. Love involves sacrifice because it necessitates giving something up, that you have to accept something else, but the compensation it brings is such that you can't call it a sacrifice. The priest here in Río de Janerio who feeds four hundred beggars a day is happy. Obviously he doesn't have a pleasant life: looking for food for four hundred beggars every day and living with them. But I do not doubt that he feels truly happy, because what for any of us would be a sacrifice, for him is not. Now, if he did that as a sacrifice, then he'd be a masochist.*

M.C. — *And that wouldn't be healthy.*

J.A. — *And he wouldn't be happy.*

M.C. – *For example, when I get confused when I'm trying to learn something and I'm told, 'Come on, repeat it! You'll see how you start picking it up,' I repeat it gladly, until I do it properly, but if they tell you, 'You're stupid!' then I leave, because they predispose you to do it badly.*

P.G. – *I'd like to get back to the concept of the journey as something that makes you freer. I see a problem, because when you're travelling it's easier to be free, search for your own identity, find yourself, and it's all very enriching, it's like feeling loved. I read a book about love called* I Love You, *and I identified that journey as a falling in love that suddenly frees you of so many things. Now then, the problem comes when you return from the journey to everyday reality. For me, the bigger effort, and what still pulls me back towards the manual – because I still feel I'm in that contradiction – is having to live alongside people who have not discovered the same things as I have. On the one hand, I'd love them to be able to discover them, but I also wonder if they have to.*

– Yes, because there's the big problem. I see it here on the beach. In the mornings it's completely deserted, a mother comes with her child and sits down, a couple of lads arrive and start playing with a ball, then some gorgeous girls looking to get a guy with their tiny bikinis, and the next mother who arrives isn't going to sit near the babes, because she'll feel a little ugly, nor near the boys playing ball, because she's not going to play; so she sits, naturally, beside the other mother. The children start playing, the hunks show up and sit near the babes. The beach starts to arrange its universe, get it? And, bit by bit, the tribes form, one of mothers with children, one of good-looking young people, the ones trying to get lucky. They form naturally, but it takes time for things to take their places in the natural organization. We can't change it, the mothers with their children are mothers with children, the sporty types want to play sports and they're happy, that's their way of worshipping God. There is a process of identification.

That's why I talk so much about the warrior of the light, where suddenly you see in someone's look that they want the same things you're looking for, and that's even though we are imperfect, with lots of problems, with our moments of cowardice. All the same we feel we're worthy, that we have the capacity for change and on we go.

It's not about convincing people, Paula, but about finding someone who is also out there feeling alone and thinking about the same things as you, understand? Am I making myself clear?

P.G. – *The problem is there are so few, or at least I haven't met very many.*

– There are lots, and it's funny how a writer or a book is, to a great extent, the catalyst. If you read Henry Miller, you'll notice you have something in common with that person, the same if you read Borges. So a book, a film, works of art in general, can have a huge catalysing effect, because they serve to help you recognize you're not alone, that there's someone who thinks like you.

J.A. – *For example, if you see a person on a plane reading a certain book, you know you can speak to her.*

P.G. – *One time, I was on a train going to Zaragoza to see my family. I was travelling with my father and my grandmother and I sat beside a young girl who had* Brida *with her. The day before I'd been at the Madrid book fair and I'd been trying to decide whether to buy* The Fifth Mountain *or* Brida *and in the end, I don't know why, I opted for* The Fifth Mountain. *When I sat down in the train, I looked at the girl who I'd never seen before in my life and at her book, and thought, 'Wow, what a coincidence, just yesterday I was looking at that exact book.' Eventually, I couldn't restrain myself and I told her and she said, 'I was wondering whether to buy* The Fifth Mountain *or* Brida.' 'The Fifth Mountain? *Look, I've got it right here in my bag.' And she turned out to be the daughter of a friend of my aunt's, who lives in Zaragoza. I started looking around for the hidden camera, because this had to be a set-up.*

– I know exactly what you mean, I've often had the feeling someone must be filming what was going on.

P.G. – *Sometimes I open the Bible at any page and start reading and it seems like it's speaking directly to me, and you think, but how can this be?*

– It's the same as what I told you about the taxi driver. That's what I thought, as if an angel is using other people's mouths.

J.A. – *But books are very significant, because if you see someone with a book you love, you can talk to that person immediately. If they're reading a book you don't know at all, you wouldn't dare, but if it's a book you know well, you realize straight away they're on the same wavelength as you.*

– Paula, are you from Zaragoza?

P.G. – *My whole family is Aragonese but Ana and I were born in Madrid.*

J.A. – *And you, María?*

M.C. – *I'm from Madrid too.*

P.G. – *I'm studying architecture and I'm very interested in art, modern art seems to have many concentrated passions and if you have the good fortune to know someone who paints, you'll see that a painting speaks very much of the emotions of people these days. What do you think of modern art?*

– I believe art is always the translation of a generation, of the feelings of a generation towards its contemporaries.

P.G. – *That's what I think too.*

– Of course, a key moment arrives when you have to separate what is art from what is fashion. I think there are many ways to tell a story and architecture is one of the most incredible, because the great history of humanity is told by architecture. There are many theories, many books about buildings, where all knowledge is reflected. And that's starting from the pyramids, by way of the Gothic cathedrals, what have you, where you can clearly see they weren't just trying to build something. There is the life of the times, the history, the beliefs and the way of trying to pass what we already know to the next generation, not a fad, but the best of ourselves. Modern art has its exaggerations. Sometimes it has very little to do with art itself, which is the capacity for touching the heart, not for navel-gazing. There is a tendency to call things art that aren't art; art is no more than transmitting to the caravan of life what we've learned along the way.

J.A. – *Basically, art is a journey.*

– Using the metaphor of the journey, I see life as a caravan: I don't know whence it came or where it's going to end up. While we travel, babies are born in the caravan and listen to their grandmother's stories and the children become grandparents and tell their part of the journey and die. History gets transmitted from generation to generation, directly to the heart, the experience of that generation; and art, in general, is our way of transmitting – to use a term from alchemy – the quintessence of things, because I can't explain to you what the world was like, when three girls from Madrid, a journalist from *El País*, a poet, another great poet, and I all got together. We can't explain that.

However, we have poetry to say it, we have painting, we have sculpture, a building, whatever you translate your emotion into. One day, your grandchildren will pass by and see what you've created from within as an architect, and they won't perceive, perhaps, the whole story, just as we can't know who picked these grapes, but they're going to enjoy it as we enjoy. That's the quintessence.

J.A. – *In my book of conversations with the philosopher Fernando Savater, he says we build and leave all these vestiges, art, architecture, all these things, because we know we have to die one day and for that reason, animals, who don't know they have to die, don't leave traces. And that's how culture is born.*

– Perhaps it's our longing for eternity that leads us to have children and build things, although I think it goes further because if not we wouldn't have artists with children, because from the moment you have children, you know you're leaving something very solid. I think we leave these things to share, because we love life, not because we're going to end, but because there's some love within us we want to share. This love fills us and, from the moment it fills us, the first thing that inspires us is the necessity of letting it be known.

A.G. – *And we also have to tell it, because we writers have that function, to recount our lives.*

– To experience them. You receive it, transform it and share it. As I said in *The Pilgrimage*, agape is the love that is more than love, and that has to be shared.

J.A. – *Now that you've mentioned it, how do you distinguish between agape and eros? Because in* The Pilgrimage *you distinguish between three types of love.*

– *Eros* is the love between two people, *filos* is the love of learning and *agape* is the love beyond the fact of liking or not liking, the love Jesus spoke of when he said: 'Love your enemies.'

We talk a lot about the enemy, the adversary, and I told Juan I can love my enemies and symbolically kill them without pity. That is my personal truth, it's my way of looking at life; I see the idea of antagonism as central to creation. Life as struggle, the good fight, is very present in *The Pilgrimage*, it's neither good or bad, it's a combat, a constant confrontation of energies, and if I make a move I affect fifty atoms or molecules, which affect others and resound in the furthest corner of the universe. Every move I make, everything I do, every thought I have is the product of a conflict between one thing and another, and that's in the basis of creation, in the moment we know as the Big Bang, the explosion at the beginning of the conflict.

When I was I can't remember how old, maybe eighteen, I read a book that made a huge impression on me: it was called *Mahābhārata*, a sacred book. A classic. This book forms part of an epic, an epic of India, its history, it was later made into a very boring movie. It's something like *Don Quixote* for you.

There's a point where there's going to be a civil war because the king left his kingdom to his nephew instead of to his son. The son protests and says he's going to fight for it. The nephew agreed: we'll do battle. There was going to be a civil war. The king, who was blind, was on a mountain top overlooking the battlefield with the two armies facing each other – his son's and his nephew's – and the battle was about to start, with the standards, warriors, bows and arrows, and such. At that moment God arrives to watch the battle. The general of one of the armies takes his carriage, leaves his army, goes to the centre of the battlefield, throws down his bow, his arrows, turns to God and says, 'How horrific! What's about to happen here is carnage, we're going to kill each other, to die, this is a civil war and there are good people on both sides. This has divided us. My master is on one side and my mother on the other, we're going to provoke a massacre. So I'm not going to fight, I sacrifice myself here.' And God answers, 'But, what do you think you're doing? You're at the start of a battle. This is not the moment to have doubts; if life places you in this position of struggle, fight, go and start the fight, later we'll discuss all these things, but at this moment you have a battle before you.'

In reality, God is saying to him: the battle you have before you is part of the movement of the world. That forms part of this healthy conflict between all the forces in the universe.

J.A. – *Or in other words, you conceive of the world in terms of a battle.*

– If you take things to their extreme, everything is conflict, but not in the sense of the battle as a bad combat, but the good fight of motion, of the things that push you towards what you were talking about now. That the journey ends and you get home and wonder, now what? And conflict is born, but it's a positive conflict, because it's what makes you keep going.

J.A. – *Do you mean you can't stop making choices.*

– You can choose between two classic paths, meditation or the good fight, but you have to choose. If you're a monk, Trappist or Buddhist or whatever, you enter a monastery and devote yourself to constant meditation, but if you're a person who needs action, you're going to be a Jesuit, a more war-like spirituality. But you have to choose between yoga of action or yoga of inaction. You can't stop, because there is no evil or good, as God said, what there is, is motion. And in the sense that there is motion, we often see things as evil or good.

J.A. – *But it's not always easy to distinguish between the forces of good and of evil.*

– When you're in combat, of course you perceive negative forces, to give them a name, and you fight against them. There is a scene in *By the River Piedra I Sat Down and Wept*, which is something that happened to me. I was in Olite, I wanted to go into the church. I was with a fantastic Spanish guide, from Zaragoza. I arrived, the door was open, I wanted to go in and a man by the door said, 'You can't go in.' 'What do you mean I can't go in?' 'No, because it's noon and it's closed.' 'Please,' I explained I wasn't from Spain, that I was only in the country for a few days, so please let me go in for five minutes. 'No, no you can't because it's twelve o'clock. It opens again at three.' I asked again, almost begging him to let me in for a couple of minutes to pray. 'No, no.' 'Why not?' I said, 'I'll go in right now, and you watch me.' Because there was no sense to it, he was there not doing anything, he was going to be there all afternoon.

That man was the symbol of the moment in which you have to say 'No' to something which is contrary to the law, to authority, to whatever. This is the moment when the figure of the adversary appears and it's the moment when the warrior symbolically kills him, the traveller kills or they kill him, for he might have been much stronger and killed me; I went through a terrible humiliation but I like combat.

J.A. – *It's similar to Jesus Christ reproaching the Pharisees when his disciples broke the Sabbath because it had been created for man, not man for the Sabbath.*

– Exactly. There are two energies in play. You are implacable, because you keep going and don't measure the consequences, you're beyond them, that leap into the abyss we were talking about, faith. I wasn't hurting that man, I wasn't keeping him from going to have his lunch or leaving. He was keeping me from entering the church only because he thought it was against the rules. I didn't accept. I forgot about law and killed him symbolically.

J.A. – *Don't you think it also has to do with the scene in the Gospels where Jesus disobeys his parents?*

– Oh yes, Jesus confronted Mary and Joseph often.

J. A. – *Something that shocks quite a few Catholics.*

– And when his mother went to see him and told them to tell him his mother was there, he answered, 'My mother? Who is my mother?'

P.G. – *I used to think that sounded like a rejection of his mother and his brothers and sisters, but I understand it's more a broadening of outlook than a rejection.*

J.A. – *No. It means to say, I have to follow a path and you can't get in my way.*

P.G. — *But it's a broadening of perspectives. I think that, probably, understood from our times, if I said that to my mother, she'd feel bad, but if she took it as a broadening of outlooks, she couldn't take it that badly.*

J.A. — *If you don't say it out of fear of hurting your mother's feelings or she stops you from following your path, that is choosing. It's what Paulo says, you have to make a choice there, you have to decide to follow your path, even though it makes your mother suffer. It's not that you don't love her, it's a conflict between the love you have for her, which you don't deny, and the love I have for myself, which makes me follow my course. In that conflict you have to decide.*

This conflict with the family is fundamental. I talk a lot in my books about the conflicts I had with my parents, which were extreme. Nevertheless, I have to thank them, because they confronted me too, and educated me, they opposed me and out of it emerged the good fight.

P.G. — *You're talking about living every moment. There is a path, but then there are also many things to experience, it's not just about following along and whatever happens happens, because in each situation you'll decide if you go into the church or not, or do you think you have to confront at all cost?*

— No, not total confrontation, you'll last a day at that and then run out of energy. That's why, in *The Fifth Mountain* you see the balance between rigour and compassion all the time, there are times when you have to say 'No' and times when you have to let yourself be led, and totally, until you see where they're taking you. That's got nothing to do with your power of decision, it's not giving up deciding; I decide whether I'm going to let myself be led, or whether I'm going to confront, but I decide, I don't stay at the crossroads.

J.A. – *Which seems to be sacred in all religions.*

– Yes, from Mercury, who was the god of crossroads. Here, in Brazil, if you go out on a Friday night, you'll see they still put food at junctions, because it's there, in all religions, where the gods look.

M.C. – *The other day, at home, we were talking about the cosmos and chaos. We were saying there is only cosmos, that chaos forms part of the cosmos, that it all makes sense. And we were talking about an example in Río, that there is a tremendous contrast between this part of the city, the rich part, and the favelas. It is an example of how chaos is also the cosmos. Even a crossroads is a cosmos, these are the critical moments you talk about. We know we have to choose one way or the other, but even staying once in the middle is making a leap, probably towards something you don't know yet, for bad or for good, but a moment like that is also important.*

And, it's realizing that, no matter how much you decide in your life, there's always something missing, and maybe it's that you're tiny and keep failing and perhaps that wasn't what you had to change at a critical moment.

– That's the problem, María. Many people ask me, 'and if such and such had happened to you in your life ...?' My dictionary doesn't contain the word 'if', the conditional. It contains I don't know how many thousands of words but 'if' isn't there; that conditional 'if' can destroy me, because at the moment I choose my path, or take a decision, I do it, it can turn out well or badly, but it is a decision. But were I to think: 'Oh, if only I'd done that ... !' then I'd ruin everything.

M.C. – *But, in my opinion, the problem is that we can decide we have to make our way, but we never know if it's good or bad. So, perhaps doubt is also something good. In the critical moment, you don't know if it's bad or good.*

– I'm sorry, María, but you're talking about trust there, doubt has nothing to do with trust. Doubt is the moment of the decision, but you trust, understand? You're going to keep having doubts all your life. I have always had them and they're getting bigger all the time, but they don't keep me from making a decision. Doubt isn't whether or not I make a mistake. Later you can reflect. What I've seen during my lifetime is that the possibility of correction always exists, there's always a second chance.

M.S. – *Thank God that chance for correction always exists.*

– Thank God!

M.C. – *But what we're talking about is after you've made that leap and taken a decision, thanks to which you had doubts, or the time before the change, when one retakes one's life. Those are doubts, crises, crossroads. Maybe not being able to do what you have in hand is what makes you search, travel, do, or provoke a conflict that leads you to find a path. Therefore, that crisis has been good.*

– Crises are always good because they are the points at which you have to make a decision.

P.G. – *I have an Italian friend who's going to come to Río, she was with me in England when I was travelling, and she said, 'I've always been obsessed with perfection, though I didn't know it. I often fooled people into thinking I was just perfect.' 'Paula,' she said to me, 'I have a classical education, I'm Roman, and you know what the word perfect means. Do you?' I told her I didn't. 'Being perfect,' she explained, 'means to be complete, and a person can't be complete without the evil part, but knowing how to keep it in check. That's being perfect.' That will free you, it will let you accept your humanity, see that you are what María was saying, your chaos and your cosmos.*

– Even Jesus, when someone said to him, 'You are good,' would get angry. 'Only God is good,' said Jesus.

M.S. – *The Chinese see the word 'crisis' as an opportunity.*

P.G. — *Before I came to Río, my boyfriend told me just that. He didn't use the word 'crisis' but 'problem'. 'Paula, the Chinese see the word "problem" as an opportunity,' he said.*

M.S. — *Paulo has talked about pilgrimages, about the way, as a search for his own identity. The question is, is it a task that gets finished at some point, or is it a permanent state? Is it an event or a process?*

— Good question, Mauro.

M.S. — *Because behind this question lies the justification, or lack thereof, for the pilgrimage.*

— Exactly. I have always tried to answer the famous question, 'Who am I?' and I'm not going to try again. It's not a question anymore, it's an answer: 'I am'. And from the moment that I am, I have to be. So, I can't answer, I have to be. It was the same answer God gave Moses when he asked, 'Who are you?' 'I am who I am,' He answered. I believe that we are, and no more, and here we are. From that moment the pilgrimage begins. I used to have goals, I still think they're very important, to have an idea, to organize your life a little, but understand that the way is the great pleasure.

M.S. — *That is, the aim is the process. It's a great frustration for many people, either by making a pilgrimage, or whatever other method of interior or exterior*

quest, they don't find the end, because they don't understand the true meaning of
beginning. We have to be very aware that here, for example, we are all, each in
our own way, searching for our own reasons. I think that all of us here under-
stand the meaning of that process, but if someone was here who didn't understand
the meaning of the process, although they might marvel at the opinions, they
would leave greatly confused.

– Yes. There's a poem by Cavafy, a fantastic Greek poet, called
'Ithaka', it's magnificent, because Ithaca is the city where Ulysses
had to get back to after the war. The poem begins: 'Setting out on
the voyage to Ithaka/You must pray that the way be long ...' And
at the end of the poem, he says: 'Poor though you find it, Ithaka
has not cheated you./Wise as you will have become with all your
experience,/You will have understood the meaning of an Ithaka.' I
think he is completely right.

When I first saw the Cathedral of Santiago it was a blow. I said
to myself, 'This is the site I was dying to get to at the beginning of
my pilgrimage, but now that it's over, I have to make a decision.'
Up until then I had it very clear in my mind that I had to make
this pilgrimage, and when I got there I thought, 'Now what do I
do? What do I do with this cathedral? What do I do with everything?' So the meaning of the voyage is in the verses of Machado,
the Spanish poet: 'Wayfarer there is no way, we make the way
by walking.'

M.S. — *I remember at Jacqueline Kennedy Onassis's funeral, her companion of her later years, her husband, from whom a speech was expected at such a solemn moment, simply read the poem 'Ithaka' which Paulo quoted.*

— Really? I didn't know that.

M.S. — *We were talking before about crossroads, about the 'Yes' or 'No', about the advance or retreat, I took a few notes and perhaps the most dangerous feeling of the way is the 'perhaps', the 'maybe', which allows for reflection at the crossroads. It's a word that paralyses, that interrupts the path and contains a reflection towards the advance or retreat, two forms of action. Paulo, you said this had nothing to do with doubt, but there are many people who believe the 'perhaps' to be a form of action. When you establish a distinction between doubt and trust, the doubt is healthy, the 'perhaps' is not healthy, it's what undoes action.*

A.G. — *The worst human drama is having to choose, because the truth is you'd like to live it all at once. But you have to choose.*

— But that's a trap, because the truth is when you choose, you live it all at once, all of it, everything. At the moment you exercise your power of decision, all the ways are already there, concentrated in this way.

A.G. — *But, when you go this way, have you not given up experiencing what might have happened over there?*

– No. This is not a metaphor, it's a reality. We spoke of the Aleph, all ways are the same way, but you have to choose and experience along the way you've chosen all the ways you haven't chosen. It's a metaphor, because you don't have to give anything up. The way you've chosen contains all the ways.

Getting back to Jesus, he said, 'My father's house has many mansions.' All ways lead to the same God. To put it in a very personal key, we have our way, it's our choice, but there could be a hundred or two hundred. The ancients said: 'There are eight or nine ways to die.' If you choose your way, it's your personal story, your destiny, your legend. What you shouldn't do is live your father's way or your husband's, because they're not your paths, and you'll get to the end of your life without experiencing your own. The others don't contain this one, but this one contains all the rest.

And now we're going to have something to eat and a little drink and then we'll carry on.

(The writer was gratifyingly impressed by the level of conversation with the three Spanish students, which ended up involving everyone present. Coelho suggested we take a break to eat some ham and cheese tapas and try a magnificent Italian wine he'd been given.)

A.G. – *I wanted to ask you if you weren't scared to have told Juan so many intimate stories of your life, because you're going to be left exposed.*

– No, I'm not afraid to expose myself, just the opposite. I believe it's a writer's obligation, it's very easy to hide behind a book and create an image that you then have to live and which pursues you. I experienced that in the music business: they imposed the role of celebrities on us, I lived it and two or three years later tragedy ensued. I promised myself I'd never be a personality. I am, but I want to be the real one, not the one they construct.

A. G. – *You're going to have to prepare yourself, because it could be a shock to many of your readers.*

– I hope so, I hope so. Jesus said it very clearly: 'The truth shall make you free.' I think the only way to be free is through truth. That infuses me with the ability to go on writing. Maybe what I'm doing with Juan, by telling him my whole life story, without hiding anything – to such an extent that I hope, after finishing this book, not to have to talk about my life again for another twenty years – won't be politically correct now, but in the long run, they'll respect me and I'll feel freer and my readers will understand it's my truth and they're going to accept me as I am, even though I'm always in a process and in motion.

P.G. – *What are you looking for when you write?*

– Myself, because I am many Paulo Coelhos and at each moment of my life I've made interior changes and I still don't understand myself completely. I also write to know who I am at this precise moment.

Then I change and I have to write another book, and so I can share my many changes, my many facets, my many hues. Insofar as I am honest and sincere – which is not at all easy, an exercise in discipline as well – I have an identity with my books, and if I have that identity with them, surely I can transmit beyond words the energy of this identity.

Perhaps the only way of explaining my international success would be that what I transmit is something that exceeds the mere words of my books. But that is hard to explain.

– If there's nothing else, I'm going to interview Juan Arias now, because I am very curious to get to the bottom of some of the things he wrote about Pope John Paul II and about the Vatican.

My conversations with Coelho continued over the next few days but I wanted the book to finish with this encounter – the conversation with his unexpected readers – as emblematic of the many young people the world over interested in the Brazilian writer's work and who often turn his books – as happened before with Castaneda's – into material for reflection in their own search for personal destiny.

Index

THE ALCHEMIST
Paulo Coelho

Every few decades a book is published that changes the lives of its readers forever. Paulo Coelho's *The Alchemist* is such a book. With over 27 million copies sold worldwide, *The Alchemist* has already achieved the status of a modern classic.

This is the story of Santiago, an Andalusian shepherd boy who dreams of travelling the world in search of a treasure as extravagant as any ever found. From his home in Spain he journeys to the exotic markets of Tangiers and then into the Egyptian desert, where a fateful encounter with the alchemist awaits him.

The Alchemist is a transforming novel about the essential wisdom of listening to our hearts, learning to read the omens strewn along life's path and, above all, following our dreams.

VERONIKA DECIDES TO DIE
Paulo Coelho

Veronika seems to have everything she could wish for. She is young and pretty, has plenty of attractive boyfriends, goes dancing, has a steady job, a loving family. Yet Veronika is not happy; something is lacking in her life. On the morning of November 11th, 1997, she decides to die. She takes an overdose of sleeping pills, only to wake up some time later in Villete, the local hospital. There she is told that although she is alive now her heart is damaged and she has only a few days to live ...

This story follows Veronika through these intense days as, to her surprise, she finds herself drawn into the enclosed world of Villete. She begins to notice more, to become interested in the other patients. She starts to see her past relationships much more clearly and understand why she had felt her life had no meaning. In this heightened state, Veronika discovers things she has never really allowed herself to feel before: hatred, fear, curiosity, love – even sexual awakening. Against all odds, she finds she is falling in love and wanting, if at all possible, to live again ...

THE DEVIL AND MISS PRYM
Paulo Coelho

A stranger arrives in the small mountain village of Viscos. He carries with him a backpack containing a notebook and eleven gold bars. He comes searching for the answer to a question that torments him: are human beings, in essence, good or evil? In welcoming the mysterious foreigner, the whole village becomes an accomplice to his sophisticated plot, which will forever mark their lives.

In this stunning new novel, Paulo Coelho's unusual protagonist sets the town a moral challenge from which they may never recover. A fascinating meditation on the human soul, *The Devil and Miss Prym* illuminates the reality of good and evil within us all, and our uniquely human capacity to choose between them.

MANUAL OF THE WARRIOR OF LIGHT
Paulo Coelho

Manual of the Warrior of Light is an invitation to each of us to live our dream, to embrace the uncertainty of life and to rise to meet our own unique destiny. In his inimitable style, Paulo Coelho helps us to discover the warrior of light within each of us.

With inspiring short passages, we are invited to embark upon the way of the warrior: the one who appreciates the miracle of being alive, the one who accepts failure and the one whose quest leads him to become the person he wants to be.

ELEVEN MINUTES
Paulo Coelho

Eleven Minutes tells the story of Maria, a young girl from a Brazilian village, whose first innocent brushes with love leave her heartbroken. At a tender age, she becomes convinced that she will never find true love, instead believing that 'Love is a terrible thing that will make you suffer ...' A chance meeting in Rio takes her to Geneva, where she dreams of finding fame and fortune yet ends up working as a prostitute.

In Geneva, Maria drifts further and further away from love while at the same time developing a fascination with sex. Eventually Maria's despairing view of love is put to the test when she meets a handsome young painter. In the odyssey of self-discovery, Maria has to choose between pursuing a path of darkness, sexual pleasure for its own sake, or risking everything to find her own 'inner light' and the possibility of sacred sex, sex in the context of love.

In this gripping and daring new novel, Paulo Coelho sensitively explores the sacred nature of sex and love and invites us to confront our own prejudices and demons and embrace our own 'inner light'.

www.harpercollins.co.uk/coelho

For the latest information on

Paulo Coelho, excerpts from his

books and exclusive competitions,

visit our website.